Grow Your Business Using Biblical Principles™

By Gilbert Pagan

Grow Your Business Using Biblical Principles™

Table of Contents

Chapter One - Introduction **6**
   About The Author 6

Chapter Two – Business Planning **8**
   An Overview of Business Plans 10
      Guidelines 12
      Main Sections 12

Chapter Three - Christian Decision Making **14**
   Types of Decisions 14
   The Seven Wisdom Signs 16
      1. Common Sense 16
      2. Spiritual Counsel 17
      3. Personal Desires 18
      4. Circumstances 19
      5. Scripture 20
      6. Fasting & Prayer 21
      7. Previous Experience 22

Chapter Four - Zacchaues the Tax Collector **24**
   Zacchaeus the Tax Collector 26
   The Miracle of the Fish 28

Chapter Five – David & Goliath **30**
   Steps To Success 30
   Business Goliaths 31
   The Story 34
   What David Did 35

Chapter Six – Getting And Using Finance 38
Funding Issues 38
Start-ups 38
Existing Businesses 40
Sources of Finance & Considerations 41
Where to Look 41
Commercial Finance 42
Private Finance 42
Equity 43
Investment vs. Loans 45
Soft Sources 45
Crowd Sourced Finance 46
Using Your Personal Assets 47
Using Barter and Exchange 47
Funding Through Cash flow 48
Tips on Raising Finance 48

Chapter Seven - Defining Your Customer 50
The CPA Story 51
Your Image 52
The Dollar Store Story 53
Narrowing Your Market 54
Testing Your Market 56
Offering a Great Service 57
Fixing the Price 58
Using Effective Advertising 60

Chapter Eight - Biblical Decision Making 62

Chapter Nine – God's Authority Given to Man 65
Using Authority in Your Business 65
The Power is Yours 66
Peter – The Number One Disciple 67

Grow Your Business Using Biblical Principles™

Chapter Ten – INC5000 72
  Tip # 1: Doing it Differently 73
  Tip # 2: Widen Your Output 74
  Tip # 3: Bang the Drum 75
  Tip # 4: Know Your Best Side 76

Chapter Eleven – Increasing B2B Sales 78

Chapter Twelve - Taking Risks 81
  Keep a Clear Head 82
  Why Risk is Good 82
  Biblical Inspiration 83
  Babe Ruth & Thomas Edison 85
  Risk Aversion 86

Chapter Thirteen - 3 Steps to Grow Your Business 87
  Step 1: Pray and Fast 87
  Step 2: Ask in the Name of Jesus 89
  Step 3: Tithe 90

Chapter Fourteen - Jesus Speaks to the Masses 93
  Introduction 93
    Jesus' Methods: Befriending and Relationships 94
  The Nature of Communication 95
  Christ's Principles of Communications 96
    Declare Peace 98
  Eat with People 98
  Take as Well as Give 99
  Pray for their Healing 99
    Declare the Kingdom 100
  Summary 101

Chapter Fifteen – How to Get More Leads...........................105
  Step 1 – Know Thy Customer 107
  Step 2 – Go Out And Seek 108
  Step 3 – Talk to Them 110
  Step 4 – Connecting Electronically 111
  Step 5 – Getting the Deal..113
  Step 6 - The Blackhole of Voicemail 116
  Step 7 – Keep Contacting 118

Chapter Sixteen – The Right Connections 120
  A Proactive Approach...120
  Profiting From Connections 122
  Avoiding Naysayers..123
  Christian Business Networks..124

Chapter Seventeen - Questions & Activities 125
  Personal..125
  Business 125

Grow Your Business Using Biblical Principles™

Chapter One - Introduction

This book is for anyone who is considering starting a business or anyone who already has an existing business. Both groups will benefit from learning how to grow their business, whether for profit or as a non-profit organization – *using Biblical Principles*.

It includes passages quoted from the Bible as illustrations, core business concepts and tips to help business owners and managers use Christian thinking in their work.

Above all, this is a success guide; by following these principles, learning the right lessons, and applying the Christian foundation every day, you can have a growing, successful business with happy clients, staff and a happy owner!

About The Author

Gil Pagan is a bi-lingual Spanish pastor and business owner in North Carolina. He also owns and operates an "INC 5000" recognized Fastest Growing private company in the U.S. Lease A Sales Rep is a national sales outsourcing company (www.LeaseASalesRep.com) that works with businesses to grow their sales by outsourcing all or part of the sales process. They help companies that have hit a brick-wall with their sales, have a breakthrough. They provide lead generation, appointment setting services and inside and outside sales teams. Gil is also the radio host of the "Grow Your Business Series Using Biblical Principles" in North Carolina.

Gil has implemented a culture of Christian values in the workplace when working with customers and employees.

The mission of Lease_A_Sales Rep is to prosper businesses and employees through the "WORKS" of "OUR" hands.

Gil has an undergraduate degree from New York University, where he also completed post-graduate work in Healthcare. He also has a Master's Degree in Theology from New Brunswick Theological Seminary.

An accomplished and dynamic speaker and preacher, Gil has led numerous conferences, seminars and workshops on sales and the integration of biblical principles to BOOST business sales growth.

Chapter Two – Business Planning

The challenging economy has affected many small businesses in service sectors like construction and the trades, including painters, electricians, remodelers and landscapers, among others. It has also drastically affected retail stores, restaurants and many others that depend on foot traffic for a large portion of their business.

For this reason, many small business owners and consultants are in the fight of their lives to stay afloat. I have some words for you in this chapter: Hold on, hold on, hold on. You are going to come out of this. God is in the midst of your situation, and you are on the verge of a breakthrough. The breakthrough is coming.

You need to have a plan for you business. I'm not talking about a business plan here, although that's very important too, but a visionary plan. Proverbs 16:3 states, *"Commit your plans to the Lord and I will affirm them"*.

Clarify your focus to begin with and ask plenty of questions. How many clients do you want? How many employees do you want working for you? What industries do you want to work in? What annual revenues would you like to have for your brick and mortar business, virtual business, MLM business, health business, etc.? Whatever it is, write that down and present it to God.

Many business owners and consultants that I speak with are absolutely phenomenal in the provision of the services that they provide. In order to expand, they need to regularly update and develop their business plans and implement better marketing strategies. They might work in car repair, as a contractor, painter or any industry, but the common theme is that the successful ones plan carefully and regularly.

Gilbert Pagan

The lesser achievers often don't know or have not spent any time determining who their target market is. Many are unfocused and running multiple businesses, none of which are profitable, and if anything, they are stealing time away from being focused on the one business that actually could be successful. How many times have you gone to a networking event and started up a conversation with someone, asked for a business card and were given two or three cards? One is for a real estate broker, the second a merchant credit card processor and the third a health drink distributor. Now, there is nothing wrong with any of these businesses, but you cannot do the three simultaneously and be successful. You need to choose one and give it all that you've got!

Again, Proverbs 16:3 states, *"Commit Your plans to the Lord and He will affirm them."*

This also means you need to be focused. In order to start and grow a business, you have to have a market in mind. Let's look at the following steps that can help you in growing your business. I will use the example of a General Contractor; someone who builds, repairs or upgrades houses or commercial properties.

Grow Your Business Using Biblical Principles™
Remember these steps and questions:

1. Is the contractor focused on Business to Business (B2B) or Business to Consumer (B2C) markets? Does he do commercial or residential property? Are his contracts valid at the state, federal, or local B2B level?
2. Who will be his clients? What types of companies will he work with - property managers, HOA's, new construction, etc.? How large should the prospect companies be, in revenue or number of employees?
3. Where will he be? In NY, FL, NC, the entire U.S.? Does he have the resources to serve the entire state or U.S.? What about employees and vehicles?
4. Now that he knows that he is looking at the B2B market, does he know his targets and geography? How will clients know that he exists? He will need to determine the best way to reach them; through associations, playing a bit of golf perhaps. He must make phone calls and radio advertising. Do you get the picture? You may need a bit of help on how to figure this out for your own business, but the principles remain constant.

You must get moving and keep moving in business. Many business owners wait until they feel the plan is perfect before they implement it. They over-analyze and get into analysis paralysis. God wants you to make a move so that He can move, and put things in place. He needs you to step out in faith so that He can step up.

I. *An Overview of Business Plans*

First of all, there is nothing that can be considered a "normal business", and for the same reason, there is no "one size fits all" business plan. Everyone has to deal with a variety of quirks, including the market, customers, time and above all, the driver of the business – YOU.

There are standard sections to a plan – ways that people have broken their ideas down into simpler chunks which have proven reliable over the years. By reading other people's plans and following a recognized template, you can get a good head start. However, you will need to fill in all the ideas and details which *only* apply to *your* vision and *your* business.

Business planning must be constant. Business plans evolve throughout the life of a business. Transitions between different stages of maturity in the business must be reflected in a changing plan which accommodates new market conditions and is flexible.

Here is a guide to the major sections a business plan must have in order to ensure you have considered the most important sections of every enterprise.

Grow Your Business Using Biblical Principles™

1. Guidelines

The Executive Summary is a short overview of the whole plan – it should be used for quick reference and most importantly, it focuses your attention on the most critical aspects of your plan itself. The Executive Summary should be as compact as possible – perhaps as little as one or two pages.

Keep it clearly focused – part of the skill in running a business is to know what not to spend time and resources on. Look at what will earn money and produce profits; everything else, everything which isn't a core function of the business has no place in your plans or your working life. The aim of any plan is growth and improvement. Keep this in mind, as every aspect of the plan and particularly the summary should reflect this aim.

If you show your plan to others, or if you are using it to raise funds, it is worth remembering to keep an eye on confidentiality. This is especially true in technology companies that rise and fall on the back of technical secrets. If your plan is going to leave the office, make sure you take out references which could compromise you. Furthermore, remember that certain sections of the plan are for management only – details like salaries, profits and sensitive information on personnel must be kept out of the wrong hands.

2. Main Sections

This is a list of important sections you will need to address thoroughly. Note that the very best plans are kept to a reasonable length. Even a huge corporation will use relatively short plans – this keeps readers from being distracted by unnecessary information.

- ➤ Executive Summary – the overview of the plan.
- ➤ Company Info – the basics of the company, structure and what it does.
- ➤ Products and Services – what you sell and where your profits come from.
- ➤ Industry – the sector you operate in and how it affects the business.
- ➤ Market – the people and companies you sell to.
- ➤ Marketing Strategy – how you will sell more and get more clients.
- ➤ Management Info – the management and their roles within the company.
- ➤ Finance – major financial data; turnover, sales revenue, predictions, etc.

There are a vast number of free resources available on the Internet, and other organizations like local business chambers or even banks can help you with model plans.

It is a good idea to read as many other business plans as you can to see how other companies have dealt with similar issues. Many model plans are available online and some companies publish parts of their plans for investment purposes. Keep your eyes open and do your research – as always.

Chapter Three - Christian Decision Making

Christian decision-making involves freedom and risk. Scripture teaches us to confirm God's moral will (as revealed in the Bible) by following certain indicators - I call them "wisdom signs". These signs are specific biblical ways that the Holy Spirit guides us in our decision-making.

This section is all about using wisdom signs in your work - to grow spiritually and grow your business. In this chapter, we will look at the type of decisions which need to be taken in your business and each of the seven wisdom signs which can help.

I. Types of Decisions

Christian decision-making can be divided into two categories. The first involves areas that are specifically addressed in the Bible. These are the revealed principles and commands of God, which must be obeyed. Those scriptural guidelines - both exhortations and prohibitions - shape our lifestyles as believers. For example, there are guidelines about stealing, murder and jealousy which can be followed with clarity.

The second category involves areas where the Bible gives no command or principle to follow. In these situations, it's the believer's responsibility to freely choose his or her own course of action within the boundaries of biblical guidelines. For example, there are passages of the Bible which deal with issues like eating, where the rules are less clear, and we need to come to our own decisions.

How do these apply to the specific decisions we face? Which church to attend, for example, or which career to pursue, or whether we're to marry and have children? Does God provide help for these life decisions beyond the general guidelines set forth in His Word?

We believe that God is a personal and loving God - not a detached, aloof being. He invites us to know Him and tells us that He has counted the very hairs of our heads. Since He's so personally involved in our lives, how then, do we understand His mind for us when we face a specific decision?

We look to the seven wisdom signs. Each one can be applied in our daily lives and reveals to us that God is active, involved in every aspect of our work and personal existence. Each sign has a Biblical origin and was found by looking directly at the words of the Lord. And each has a business application, so these are very useful tools, both spiritually and practically.

II. The Seven Wisdom Signs

Scripture describes the following seven "wisdom signs". These indicators can help you discover and affirm the Lord's will for your life.

1. Common Sense

God created people with a natural ability to make sound judgments based on facts. It's a form of wisdom that's part of God's grace to humans everywhere (Proverbs 1:1-3; 3:5-6; 4:11). My oldest boy, David, often says common sense is not so common.

When it comes to selecting a mission experience, common sense tells you to compare things like the mission organization's purpose, programs, leaders, supervision, fields, and costs. It causes you to look at your own abilities, experiences, and spiritual gifts.

Common sense in business means choosing the most effective option, looking for clarity instead of complexity and trusting in old-fashioned wisdom. Remember that business is a series of simple principles, decisions and actions which looks terrifyingly complicated from the outside but when broken down, it's simply a set of basic activities.

Common sense works as a "wisdom sign" as long as it harmonizes with the moral will of God and does not contradict what He has already revealed in Scripture.

2. Spiritual Counsel

The book of Proverbs teaches us that there is balance and wisdom in seeking the wise counsel of mature believers (*Proverbs 10:23; 15:22; 19:20; Heb. 13:7, 8*). These may include parents, close friends, teachers, pastors, or others in spiritual leadership. The Christian corrective to the extremes of individualism is the wisdom and support of the Christian community - the church - of which you are a member.

If the advice of certain counselors conflicts at points, evaluate the reasoning behind their differing viewpoints. Keep in mind the strong points of each type of counselor: your parents probably know you best; teachers and professional counselors can help you uncover conceptual blind spots you've overlooked; pastors and other spiritual counselors can put facts and situations into proper spiritual perspective.

Seeking the counsel of Bible-based Christian believers that have experience in the business world is a method that I have used to sort through decisions that were tough, but needed to be made. Those who are business owners or managers can assist in figuring out the best way to move forward.

Often, you will need to network to seek out the very best people to advise you, but any effort will be well rewarded. You need to keep an open mind in business and be ready to be wrong. Accepting mistakes, learning from others and allowing external opinions into the mix are crucial for success.

3. Personal Desires

Spiritual growth makes a significant impact on your personal desires. The psalmist wrote that when you delight in the Lord, He gives you "the desires of your heart" (*Psalms 37:4; Proverbs. 19:21; 21:21*).

As you mature, so does your business or company that you work for; your motives and desires should reflect God's desires. But your personal desires are never authoritative and must always be judged against God's Word. When two options you are considering seem truly equal, this wisdom sign tells you to choose the one you would enjoy most - follow your heart!

Desire is important in business. Firstly, it drives sales. Customers must desire your product or service before they will buy it, and as such, you need to get used to creating desire, making your business a must-have, a want, a need. Secondly, desire drives your own passion which in turn powers the business. Enterprise is tough as it is, and if you also own the business you work at, it is even tougher. To get through all the scrapes, you need a large helping of desire.

Desire also involves clarity of purpose. By thinking about what you want from your business and what your customers want from you, you can use desire to set the working parameters of the business. Often, it isn't the obvious needs that awaken desire; people don't desire the cheapest product, they want the best or the easiest to use. Others don't run their business for huge profits or in hopes of taking over the world, their desire and their pleasure comes from helping people or improving the environment.

4. Circumstances

The situation and context in which you will find yourself become vital ingredients in your decision-making process. Carefully analyze your situation (*Proverbs 16:9, 33; 20:24*).

As you contemplate your business, your situation will include factors like time, people, cost, travel, and so on. Every option has its advantages and disadvantages, similar to the decisions that need to be made in life. Try to discern the more subtle consequences of your decisions.

Writing down an idea can be an antidote to emotionalizing your decision or becoming a victim of your own impulsiveness. Rather than looking at your circumstances to analyze them and then trying to make logical decisions based on that analysis, bring it to God and pray.

Circumstances, like details, are also important in a business. Your customers' situations, their budgets and even their area and living environments all have an impact on your bottom line. Internally, the work environment, your liquid capital, credit at the bank and the general feel of the business will all affect people and your figures.

The trick is to consider everything, work it out on paper and adapt. By adapting your thinking, you will solve challenges which have stumped you for months. By adapting your products and services to your customers' circumstances and by being sensitive to their changing needs, you will increase sales. And last but certainly not least, by looking at yourself, your employees and even the country or the world as a whole, you can adapt your whole business to the changing times.

5. Scripture

God's moral will is objective, complete, and adequate as revealed in His Word. Yet the Bible does not tell us the precise answer to every situation. What it does tell us is that we must acquire wisdom and apply it to our decisions (*Proverbs 6:20-23; 8:10-11, 32-33; 9:10*).

We've all had ideas pop into our heads. Those inner impressions can come from a variety of sources - God, Satan, past experience, stress, the flesh, immaturity, indigestion, insomnia - and must be judged by God's Word. After thoughtful consideration, you may conclude that an impression or feeling is actually a good plan - a wise way to serve God - or you may decide it's foolish and ought to be ignored.

The Scripture guides us, and by studying the Bible and looking at ways that the right conduct and correct attitude have benefitted people over the ages, we can learn how to manage our business both with Biblical and Christian principles at the heart and be on the right path towards success.

For every lesson in this book, there are a hundred others waiting to be discovered in the Bible and in the wider Christian community of texts and oral tradition.

6. Fasting & Prayer

Believe it or not, this part will be radical for most Christians. The concept involves getting on your knees, while fasting and praying, to connect with God at a higher level. Fasting and Prayer is your means of communicating with God to understand His mind and His guidance. In most decisions, this is where the battle is fought (*Ephesians. 6:18*). Most people would rather eat and do other things than sacrifice the body and sacrifice their time to be with God. When a believer does this, it is viewed as a holy act of submission to God and it allows you to seek and get direct answers from God about your particular situation. I encourage those that want to see a RADICAL transformation of a situation to fast and pray. It is HIGHLY recommended. My wife and I practice this as well, fasting in the beginning of each year in January. Bring all your goals for the year in your business and personal life to God. If possible, during fasting and prayer, also give a sacrificial financial offering to the church as part of this process. Do this and you will see incredible results.

Business decisions are often made by the business owner, manager, or front line employee within the business structure. Logic is often used when making these decisions, but another powerful tool that should be used is prayer, often overlooked and forgotten.

I don't mean to imply that you should be sitting down and praying for hours before you make an initial small decision, but a quick prayer, such as "Holy Spirit, please direct me in the decisions that I need to make today, and Lord let your will be done". Simple, short and effective!

The time you spend thinking and gathering information about a decision should be matched with daily conversations in prayer. At times, it helps to focus these prayers by writing them down. I have known people who agonize over major decisions, but spend less than five minutes a day praying about them. If you are trusting God as your loving Father, doesn't it make sense that He is eager to answer your requests for wisdom through the intimate channel of prayer?

Fasting also allows for the cleansing of the mind and spirit and allows for a divine connection with God through bodily sacrifice. I have often fasted for weeks at a time for specific business issues, and have seen God move mountains in my favor. **Fasting & Prayer works!**

What business wouldn't benefit from a few hours, or even better, a few days of quiet contemplation? Numerous studies have shown that the relaxed, calm appraisal of situations and disasters in business is the best way to move forward. Pressurized, hasty decisions made in the blink of an eye are often the ones companies later regret. Set aside regular time to sit down and think, to plan and to investigate; this doesn't need to be a formal process, but it must become a regular habit.

7. Previous Experience

Life is a classroom, and you don't want to return to second grade if you can help it! Be smart. Reflect on your past decisions - and those of others - to learn how they were good for you and how they were bad (*Proverbs 10:24; 21:1*). Write down any critical decisions that influence where you are now and what options you have before you.

Romans 8:28 says that God is at work in every decision you make as a Christian committed to His will. This means that when you make the best decision possible, you can trust Him to work out the results for good.

The great news is that the business world is overflowing with examples, with gurus and experts to learn from and with statistics and data which can inform any decision. From business books to training seminars, to simply observing the masters at work, we can all learn valuable lessons the easy way.

Of course, the other aspect of using previous experience is an internalized one – the hard lessons learned by making mistakes and the others of giving birth to a healthy operation. The key to learning from mistakes is to keep calm and look at things with a wise, detached eye. These lessons are often the best, because once learned, the pain of the original experience keeps us from lapsing into old ideas and wrong methods.

Chapter Four - Zacchaeus the Tax Collector

In this chapter, I'm going to talk to you about "the influence of the Christian Business Owner", how it impacts the community and then tie it all into the Word. So get ready to hop on this train because it's leaving the station and I don't want to lose you as I move through the important story of Zacchaeus the tax collector.

If you own a home or have a job through an employer, you are probably paying taxes. The employer pays taxes, as does the employee. As homeowners, we also pay taxes, and in some states, you may have to pay an annual fee which is a tax for your vehicle.

The tax department knows every person that is an employee, has a home or vehicle, because they are paying taxes and they have your name and address, so that they can send you a bill. It doesn't matter whether you are rich or poor, fat or skinny, pretty or ugly, we all pay taxes. It is part of giving our share to support city infrastructure, fire, police services and to help those less fortunate with social services.

This is our influence at work and one of the many diverse ways we impact everything around us. For the Christian business owner, our influence can spread both the Word of God and also publicize and share the lifeblood of our businesses. To find your business influence, look around. Who do you know? Where do you shop? Where do you hang out? Which friends of friends could you contact? You'll soon see that your business influence and network of contacts are vast.

- It is often said that there are only 6 degrees of separation between you and any other person on Earth. By networking, chaining together contacts and really digging deep – it is possible to get your business and your ideas in front of *anyone*. Look at the many people who have started with nothing but are now household names. That is the power of influence.

At the time of writing of this book, we have just completed the 2010 census; wouldn't it be nice that when the census taker, who by the way also knows who you are, came to your door with a tax collector who hands you a check and tells you that you were overcharged. He then goes on to humbly apologize and hands you back a check which is your money WITH interest! Hallelujah, the heavens would open up, a bright light would come down, you would start hearing heavenly songs, etc. OK—let's snap back to reality…

That's what happened with Zacchaeus the tax collector when he met Jesus. He gave money back to the people, with another, higher purpose. Look at *Luke 19:1-10* to investigate.

Grow Your Business Using Biblical Principles™

I. Zacchaeus the Tax Collector

Luke 19:1-10

[1] Jesus entered Jericho and was passing through. [2] A man was there by the name of Zacchaeus; he was a chief tax collector and was wealthy. [3] He wanted to see who Jesus was, but being a short man he could not, because of the crowd. [4] So he ran ahead and climbed a sycamore-fig tree to see him, since Jesus was coming that way.-

[5] When Jesus reached the spot, he looked up and said to him, "Zacchaeus, come down immediately. I must stay at your house today." [6] So he came down at once and welcomed him gladly.

[7] All the people saw this and began to mutter, "He has gone to be the guest of a 'sinner.' "

[8] But Zacchaeus stood up and said to the Lord, "Look, Lord! Here and now I give half of my possessions to the poor, and if I have cheated anybody out of anything, I will pay back four times the amount."

[9] Jesus said to him, "Today salvation has come to this house, because this man, too, is a son of Abraham. [10] For the Son of Man came to seek and to save what was lost."

So that's the story of Zacchaeus.

Imagine him being in the tree and Jesus calling him out; it's like being at the super bowl with thousands of people, all followers of Jesus, there to see Him. Sitting way up at the top of the stadium, in the nose bleed section, is Zacchaeus - all 4.5 feet of him - and Jesus calls him out (or your favorite sports player calls you by name to come and sit down on the team bench).

Think of how excited you would be!

Realize this is actually happening to each of us. God is calling us to be with him.

The way Jesus called out for Zacchaeus was very special to me. It was interesting to learn that Jesus picked the business man who was taking money from everyone else and called to him. He had a legitimate business. Jesus did not just call the sick, the tired, and the poor to come to him; He called the man that was taking money from the people of Jericho and who was very wealthy. Jesus met him where he was at - in the tree. This event was very powerful.

And as the scripture says in Luke 19:8

> [8] *But Zacchaeus stood up and said to the Lord, "Look, Lord! Here and now I give half of my possessions to the poor, and if I have cheated anybody out of anything, I will pay back four times the amount."*

- Good business isn't about greed, despite what Gordon Gecko of the movie "Wall Street" used to say. Good business is a mutual exchange, and often the more you put in, the more you receive in output.

So Zacchaeus, the business owner and tax collector, gave back to all those that he had taken taxes from. And to those that he had overcharged, he gave them back their money with interest. In light of this, he was still a very wealthy man.

They did not have banks, checks, electronic transfers, Western Union, or anything like that back in those days, so he went from door to door, giving back the money he had taken. He knew everyone in town, knew where they lived. Zacchaeus was a very powerful man and now he had a different disposition.

He was now coming with a smile, love, and a lot of grace, carrying money.

How would you receive someone that smiles at you, treats you with love, and gives you some money? I could receive that all day. He was able to communicate a message of salvation to those that opened the door, and the door was opened because of who he was, a business owner and tax collector.

- Business owners have tremendous influence and Christian business owners have even more because of who we have behind us. Many of us are called by God to impact our communities through our businesses. Zacchaeus was a business owner, knew everybody by name and where they lived.

II. The Miracle of the Fish

This is a very interesting story in the context of business. This miracle was all about abundance and belief, and for the business owners out there reading this, there are some great lessons to be learned. The first thing to notice is that without belief, there was no fish.

- Business owners need faith badly. To begin with, they have a vision and a view of the world which is new. Most of the time, no one else can see it, and so faith is needed to overcome the objections, the apathy and the hurdles to make the dream reality. Also, business is full of ups and downs. When the mortgage company calls in a loan or when your cash flow is shot to pieces, you need a good heaping of faith to carry you through.

You must believe in yourself and in the power of your business and your ideas. Without this faith, confidence is impossible and the market will sense that you are not 100% sure of your commitment to being successful.

The second big lesson is to listen to the signals, keep your ear to the ground and don't become blinded by your normal routine. The fisherman didn't listen to Jesus the first time and the result was the usual dicey catch, in this case nothing. But when they heeded the call and realized something new was on the horizon, they were rewarded. *John 21:6*

- In business, you must keep your eyes open constantly. It isn't just circling competitors or tax men you need to be on your guard for, but you must also be open to opportunities. Finding and leveraging opportunity is the best way to grow a business.

Grow Your Business Using Biblical Principles™

Chapter Five – David & Goliath

In order to grow your business you have to have a plan. In *Proverbs 16:3*, it states, "Submit your plans to the Lord and I will affirm them!" It does not say when I get to it, kind of sort of, maybe so; it says "I **will** affirm them". The challenge for many business owners is to stay focused and have a plan that they can implement. You read this in a prior chapter, and it's worth repeating with another twist. In the bible, God often repeats things in order to make a point so you won't miss it.

I. Steps to Success

There are 5 points you need to cover in order to grow your business. This is really the distilled wisdom of many years, the vital areas you must consider are below. To succeed you need to ask the right questions of yourself, of the market and of your customers:

1. What type of business are you? The first step is identifying this yourself. Are you seeking a business to make a lot of money? Or to have job security? Or to have power and control? Are you a business to business (B2B) or a business to consumer (B2C) business or both? Commercial or residential? The more initial research you put into your business the further you will go over the long haul.

2. Who will be your clients? What industries will you work in? What types of companies or consumers will you work with? How large should the companies be in revenue or number of employees, etc?

3. ==Geography: where will you do your work?== What states, cities, metro markets? Do you have the resources?

4. ==How will you market your business?== How will you secure customers?

5. ==Lastly, just start.== Modify along the way as you learn what will work and what will not. Change pricing as needed. See what people will buy, how fast they will buy and what they will pay.

II. Business Goliaths

Many Christian business owners that I talk with are struggling with many issues. They tell me they can't find customers, people will not return their calls, the prospects (or potential customers) that they are talking too are not making decisions and inevitably, things have gotten slow.

Some have issues with hiring the right staff. It's hard to find good, hard-working people, and others have collection issues which lead to cash flow problems. Some have customers, but the profit is just not there. Many business owners feel they are up against a Goliath, and they are the David.

These Goliaths repeat themselves time and time again. The most common complaints are:

1. The Goliath of competition: that you are in a crowded marketplace with many other companies doing what you do.

2. The Goliath of lack of sales: that you don't know how to sell your services, you have the passion, the know-how, but not the strategic ability to make it happen.

Grow Your Business Using Biblical Principles™

3. The Goliath of the lack of financing to make the business come to life, or to stay alive.

4. The Goliath of people: finding the right people to put on your bus, and the need to get some of the current people off the bus, so you can get to where you are going with the business.

Always remember though, that these Goliaths are not insurmountable. They are only temporary; your current situation is not your destiny.

For those of you who are intimately connected to God (what I mean is that is you are fasting and praying) and serving others. You need to be very aware of all that surrounds you. When you serve others by laying hands on people and they get healed, when you pray that mountains are moved and they get moved, when you pray for a release from bondage and people are released, realize that you are a threat to the enemy, and he will try to stop you from doing what you need to do to be prosperous and successful—to get you "unfocused" so you will stop what you are doing. This can be a Goliath.

For those of you who are not as connected, God is using these challenging times to draw you closer. Because many believers are crisis oriented, they only draw close while in crisis, and move on during the good times. However, it is through the good times when you need to be stronger, so that you don't get knocked out in the tough times.

1. Competition is always around us and often, business appears challenging, which is a major Goliath on the way to crush us. Remembering how David faced up to his challenge, and setting our sights on victory despite the size of our enemies or the weight of their wallets and resources

is vital to success.

2. Some of the biggest success stories of the last decade have come from people in bedrooms taking on major corporations. Look at how Michael Dell grew from his backyard into a billionaire – despite IBM that was at the time, one of the largest and most advanced corporations of all time.

III. The Story of David & Goliath

This is a perfect story to share in a business context.

In *1 Samuel 17*, David is sent by his father Jesse to bring some food to his brothers who were on the front line in a battle against the Philistines; David was the youngest of 3 brothers.

Verse 17: *Now Jesse said to his son David, "Take this ephah of roasted grain and these ten loaves of bread for your brothers and hurry to their camp. ^{18}Take along these ten cheeses to the commander of their unit. [e] See how your brothers are and bring back some assurance [f] from them. ^{19}They are with Saul and all the men of Israel in the Valley of Elah, fighting against the Philistines."*

So Jesse gets to the camp and the camp is set in a Valley, with a mountain to the left and a mountain to the right. And let me tell you something here, **timing is everything**! Just as he gets there early in the morning to bring the food to his brothers, the Philistine Giant came out and did what he did for 40 days straight. Saying in verse 23(*1 Sam: 17:*23). Read this chapter and verse in the bible.

As Jesse was talking with them, Goliath, the Philistine champion from Gath, stepped out from his lines and shouted his usual defiance, and David heard it. "Is there any man powerful enough, strong enough, with enough courage and skill to take me on?" shouted Goliath.

God will sometimes place you in a situation where you will have to make a move. God set up David for this moment. Goliath was coming out every morning for 40 days, shouting the same defiance at the Israelites, and David was there at the same time he came out. Under normal conditions, he would have just dropped off the food and left to go back home.

- You maybe facing obstacles in your life and in your businesses. And every morning, when you wake up, you are confronted with the same situation (that same GOLIATH): where am I going to find more customers, how am I going to get more financing for my business, how am I going to resolve this legal situation, how am I going to get out of debt, how am I going to find the right people to get on the bus to help my business grow?

These fears are obstacles, those anxieties are obstacles. Some are placed there by God, and some are placed there by the enemy. Goliath struck fear and anxiety into the minds of the Israelites, in 1 Sam: 17: 24 says, when the Israelites saw the man, they all ran from him in great fear.

IV. What David Did

But David did not run. When he heard what Goliath said and saw that no one responded, he asked who is this non-believing, uncircumcised, heathen that attempts to take away our victory, our blessing, our rights to this land. This was a kid, 4 foot 7, and Goliath was 9 feet tall.

Sometimes, God will set you up; that's right it's a set-up, to see if you will make a move. The enemy will also set you up to see if you make a move. So David said, in today's lingo or vernacular, "Oh no, you didn't go there. I know you didn't just step out and threaten me and my people. It's on now! Step to the line, that's right, because we going to get busy. Because them are fighting words."

Grow Your Business Using Biblical Principles™

So David went to a brook and took 5 stones and his staff and stepped to the line to confront Goliath.

Verse 41-47 states that the Philistine (Goliath), with his shield bearer in front of him, kept coming closer to David. *^{42}He looked David over and saw that he was only a boy, ruddy and handsome, and he despised him. ^{43}He said to David, "Am I a dog, that you come at me with sticks?" And the Philistine cursed David by his Gods. ^{44} "Come here," he said, "and I'll give your flesh to the birds of the air and the beasts of the field.*

David said to the Philistine, "You come against me with sword and spear and javelin, but I come against you in the name of the LORD Almighty, the God of the armies of Israel, whom you have defied. ^{46}This day the LORD will hand you over to me, and I'll strike you down and cut off your head. Today I will give the carcasses of the Philistine army to the birds of the air and the beasts of the earth, and the whole world will know that there is a God in Israel. ^{47}All those gathered here will know that it is not by sword or spear that the LORD saves; for the battle is the LORD's, and he will give all of you into our hands."

Then Goliath started to make a move. He moved closer to David. He started to step over that imaginary line, so David took a slingshot with one of the stones he had gathered. As he starts to swing the rock, he says, I may be small, but I am mighty. That competition that you have doesn't have anything on you. They may be bigger, but I got someone bigger on my side.

As he swings the rock, Goliath steps closer. That financial problem you are facing may seem like a huge mountain, 9 feet tall, but Jehovah Jireh is your provider. Goliath stepped closer to David, David still swinging that rock and Goliath laughing at him all the same, "You think your business has a chance in this challenging economy?"

David, still swinging the rock, says, "You don't know the faith I have in God that He will supply all my needs according to his riches and Glory." So David finally let go of the rock and down went the mountain, down went the Goliath, down went that situation that kept you up at night, down went the fear and anxiety. Then David fed Goliath's carcass to the birds of the air. That is what God will do to your enemies.

- And all the spectators, the business men, the business women, your competitors, your family, your so-called friends, who are looking to see what is going to happen with your business; I tell you that rock, your faith, is traveling fast, and when it hits that situation, right in between the eyeballs, that Goliath, that Mountain and that situation will come down. People will be amazed when you step out of this situation, you are still standing, and the Goliaths are out cold, they will be amazed that you made it through the battle and that you took down the mountain.

One of those mountains that business owners face is getting financing, getting the old mighty green dollar, to help them start-up, expand, and stay open.

Grow Your Business Using Biblical Principles™

Chapter Six – Getting And Using Finance

Finance drives every business. You will use financing at all stages in the life of your company. At startup, funding is essential for getting stock, equipment and expenses covered before profits and cash flow can supply your needs. During growth, capital is needed for expansion, for financing purchase orders and for leasing equipment.

I. Funding Issues

Finding funding isn't easy. In fact, a lack of funding is the number one contributor to business failure in the USA. This can prevent a new enterprise from ever getting off the ground, can cause problems during growth, and a withdrawal of capital can bankrupt even the sturdiest business.

1. Start-ups

In the initial stages, the main problems with funding are related to a lack of a track record and uncertainty over the future of the business. Because a new venture is untried, it is difficult for a lender to make an informed decision about credit worthiness. Imagine visiting a bank to describe a new business idea. For the loan officer at the bank to be comfortable lending money to the business, he or she will need confidence that repayments will be made.

The first thing a lender will look for is cash flow and profits with which to service the loan. Most new businesses, unless they are a takeover of an established enterprise, do not have established revenues.

The way to give financial organizations confidence without actual cash flow is through a high-quality business plan and sound financial predictions. By analyzing possible sales and setting these against possible costs, a good business plan will show a funder what revenues can be expected from a business. The more evidence in the plan to back up sales forecasts and projections, the more the lender can rely on external validation of your predictions.

For example, a new bakery may produce a business plan to show their lender. This includes research on other bakeries, customer surveys to establish a market, and a set of financial projects which show how many loaves, cakes and sundries the bakery is expected to sell. Against these potential profits, the plan also shows the cost of equipping the bakery, ongoing overheads and deductions for taxes and expenses. If the lender sees that there is strong evidence that enough profit will be generated to cover a startup loan, he will be minded to approve the request.

The second aspect a lender will look for is assets against which to secure any loan. Just as a mortgage lender will look for the security of the house itself, so business lenders will look for ways to protect their investment. This could either be personal security in your own home or property or business security where a building or a piece of machinery is used to protect the loan. In the event of problems preventing normal repayments of any funding, the lender can sell the asset which secures the loan to repay the amount borrowed.

Most new businesses are unlikely to have assets; moreover, loans are often necessary to buy assets at startup stage. This creates a kind of circular problem where lenders will only loan money to a business which already has the things required to secure the loan.

Grow Your Business Using Biblical Principles™

The solution for the new business is often in the form of a personal guarantee. This is usually a kind of mortgage against property, or against other investments and assets held personally.

2. Existing Businesses

Existing businesses have advantages when raising finance, but these are balanced by some particular issues which need consideration by established operations. The principle advantage of an existing business is that revenue is normally flowing, and predictions of ability to repay loans are easier with accounts and books to extract figures from.

It should be noted that even existing businesses require thorough planning to pass finance tests. Business plans, evidence, research and financial analysis are still essential to the process. The only difference is that these rely on actual data rather than primarily on predictions.

Existing businesses have other advantages, one of which is an increased range of methods of finance. For example, an existing business can raise finance by selling the money owed to it by clients using accounts receivable finance packages. An existing business can also raise finance by using factoring. With factoring, your invoices are paid by the finance company that then collects payment from clients

One major issue for existing businesses looking to raise money is that if problems have arisen with cash flow and other elements which financiers examine when deciding investments or loans – these are glaringly apparent from financial records. A startup has yet to make mistakes. Thus, a business that needs finance to get itself out of a hole has the problem that the circumstances surrounding the funding are a reason not to fund the operation for a lender.

For example, if an overstretched air-conditioning business has repeated financial problems – issues paying suppliers, court judgments for nonpayment and ongoing cash flow difficulties – these might be solved by raising money to pay for new equipment or personnel, to make up for the lack of resources. However, a financier will be more interested in the risks shown by the present situation than a hypothetical scenario where cash flow is improved after investment.

The more efficient, successful, profitable and well administered the business, the greater chance it has of obtaining funding. It is an established truth that success begets success. In the finance world, the more responsibly and effectively you manage your business's finances, the more funding there will be. Businesses often grow by leveraging funding opportunities one after another. Funding should always be thought of as a positive investment rather than a means to solve negative issues in the business.

Finally, in the course of years in business, companies acquire assets and other securities through their cash flow and profits. When these are applied to a business plan for funding, they can be used to secure investments.

II. Sources of Finance & Considerations

There are many sources of commercial finance and investment. The most common corporate sources are commercial finance brokers, investment funds and angel groups and banks. The most common private sources are the immediate social and family circle of owners, employees and wealthy individuals.

1. Commercial Finance

A massive industry has grown up to service the needs of businesses seeking finance. The most likely part to become

Grow Your Business Using Biblical Principles™

entwined with a new or growing business is the finance broking sector. Here, a broker will have access to a whole range of finance options from different lenders, with a variety of conditions and interest rates. The broker will help the business choose the best type of funding for particular circumstances and try to negotiate the best possible deal.

Commercial lending might also be done through banks, via accountants and through online sources of commercial funds.

2. Private Finance

Private finance is very common, especially for startups. Typical sources of private finance are the owners of the business, their family and friends and high net worth individuals who either invest singly or as part of a group of investors, often called business angels.

Private finance is less formal than approaching corporate lenders or investors. Procedure may be more relaxed and it is often easier to work with a more flexible private lender or investor than a bank or institution which is very rigid and demanding in approach.

Note that typically, a private investor or financier will ask for the same types of return and security as a corporate institution. In fact, the process of raising finance privately is identical, except that the source of funds is actually a person.

3. Equity

Equity is the inherent value of a business. In financial terms, equity is usually expressed by shareholdings. Thus, if I own half the shares in a business, I also own half the equity. Equity has an important part to play in funding arrangements. There are two components to the value of a business to an investor:

1. The day to day cash and profits generated by the business, and immediate benefits which can be repaid to an investor; and

2. The long-term value of the business itself. For example if a business is eventually sold, profit is released but not through customers buying or sales of products – it is the actual organization which is sold.

The first type of value – profits and or loan repayments – is usually governed by a loan agreement. The second type of value – intrinsic value in the business – is usually governed by equity. In essence, equity decides who owns and controls a business. Many investors will want equity in exchange for taking the risk of loaning or investing money.

This means that if someone invests in your business, they may ask for ownership of a portion or share of the business and may also get some form of control over the business as a result of their ownership. For example, a new online business might get an investment from a rich private investor and some employees might put up money in the hope of making profits in the future. Each investor asks for a share in the business, proportional to their investment. This leaves the owner of the business with funds, but at the expense of shares of ownership.

Grow Your Business Using Biblical Principles™

This has two consequences. First of all, if the business is sold, profits are given out according to shareholdings. Second, and more importantly in the short term is that the business may not be under total control of the owner. Shareholdings and investments usually come with rights attached. For example, the right to vote at board meetings or the right to make certain kinds of decisions which affect the company's future.

Each investment involving equity is therefore a balancing act for a business owner. The more that is invested by outsiders, the more outside control there will be of the business. Sometimes it may be in an owner's interest to actually look for less investment to retain the control they want.

4. Investment vs. Loans

In most cases, investment and loans are two different ways of raising money. Normally, a loan comprises a sum made available to the business, secured against an asset and repayable at a profit for the lender. An investment, however, is not normally directly repayable and is designed to yield a profit when the business grows and is sold.

It is important to clearly differentiate between these two types of funding and see the differences within each model. Every type of loan or investment has a unique set of characteristics and can be compared with market norms. Ensuring the best deal for your business requires careful selection of the right investment and the right rates and conditions for borrowing money.

In the same way as different mortgages can have markedly different effects on the health and strength of a household, investments or loans and their terms can also seriously influence business life. Many financial packages are long-term and problems can stretch for many years.

5. Soft Sources

Finance is a tough industry, full of rules and possible tripwires for the unwary. There are, however, some limited sources of softer finance. These have less onerous conditions attached, may be easier to apply for and are a gentler way to fund a business. For example, federal and state assistance for businesses may provide security or direct investment on soft terms to help stimulate growth.

In some specialized types of businesses, donations and gifts may provide funding. For instance, a new veterinary clinic may find funding from animal lovers, or from organizations that have funds available to help animal welfare.

6. Crowd Sourced Finance

Crowd sourcing is really a modern extension of the old idea of small shares making up a large business. Some companies have used social media and other mass marketing techniques to attract hundreds and thousands of small investors who combine their contributions to fund a sizeable operation.

Crowd sourcing of finance also has the advantage of being a form of premarketing and market preparation. Often, the people who fund crowd sourced projects are potential clients and people with a passion or interest in the new business and the industry it is being established within. For example, a new company which makes sports equipment might find funding from the community of sports lovers, athletes and other interested parties. These are the very same people who would buy from the company once it is established.

Google is a classic example of this. When the company sold shares, millions of Internet users bought them, and the resultant publicity and spread of word of mouth is one of the reasons the company came to dominate the market after it used the funds it raised.

7. Using Your Personal Assets

As we have seen in the case of new businesses or in cases where conventional, outside funding sources are not available, an owner must sometimes be prepared to dig deep into his own pockets and assume the risk of funding an enterprise.

Taking a good look at possible ways to move money into your business can often yield a surprisingly large sum. As well as actual cash and money in bank accounts, investments can be liquidated, for example, by selling shares owned in another company, or by redeeming bonds. This allows a very direct, immediate injection of cash.

Private individuals can also borrow money in their own name. Thus overdrafts, credit cards and personal loans are often used to finance businesses. Care must be taken because the onus to make repayments of personal loans or borrowings is as strong as with commercial finance. There is no new money created and debts always need repayment. It might also be noted that personal customers offer to pay higher rates than businesses for financing so it is worth shopping around and comparing options.

8. Using Barter and Exchange

Look at the reasons you need investment and examine if there is another way to obtain what you need, without direct payment. Many businesses use flexible barter and exchange to make indirect investments. For example, if your business needs a marketing overhaul and a marketing company needs your businesses vehicle hire service, it may be possible to make a swap. Look at the people who would supply your needs and see if there is a fit between the skills, services and products in your business.

9. Funding Through Cash Flow

Perhaps the most valued type of investment and funding is derived from cash flow. Using internal resources might be difficult, especially for larger lump sums, but it is the least risky and easiest option to implement as there are no outside hoops to be jumped through.

Most sensible business owners try to build up a war chest over time which can be used for expansion, emergencies or simply to smooth out cash flow. In fact, the stronger the cash flow is within a business, the less need there may be for investments at all. Some businesses are able to grow organically through their own efforts and don't require large investment chunks to solve problems.

Of course, razor thin margins, competition and economic conditions often make it impossible to save during the normal course of operations. There is a need for both discipline and also extra effort to achieve any meaningful, self-generated investment plan.

III. Tips on Raising Finance

All finance involves business planning. The most important beneficiary of these plans is you as the owner. The figures within your plan should inform you of both how much you need to raise, which measure of investment is needed, and also how much you can afford to pay. There must be a direct, beneficial relationship between these factors which gives balance to the business.

Every investment plan must have clear objectives. Ensure that you truly understand why you are seeking funding, how you intend to use the funds as efficiently as possible and how you will generate the most possible returns from any investment.

Raising finance and providing a vehicle for investment are long-term games. There is rarely a quick buck to be made and the experts in these fields are established financial institutions who often have hundreds of years of know-how to draw upon.

Raising finance is very labor intensive. Initially, a lot of planning and research is needed to find funders and present the best possible business case for an investment. Moreover, servicing loans and satisfying investors can be resource heavy. For these reasons, it is wise to keep financial applications as lean as possible and use them sparingly, as they may form a distraction from core business processes.

Finance is a legal minefield so it is essential to read terms and conditions with extreme caution and use outside, expert advice from lawyers and accountants if you can afford them. Mistakes in finance can be very costly.

Chapter Seven - Defining Your Customer

In the previous chapters, we discussed David and Goliath and the mountain that needed to be moved in your business. Was it finances, was it competitors, was it staff? Did it involve getting people off the bus, then the right ones on? Or was it anxiety or legal issues? If you know the story of David and Goliath, David won the battle because he chose to step up, step to the line to confront the mountain, and he was victorious.

In this chapter, I want share with you how to define your customer. One of the biggest mistakes that business people make is that they want to be everything to everyone. When we cast our net too wide, we have failed to define our customer.

Business people need to ask two questions:

- Based on my product or service, who is or should be my customer?
- What is the most effective way of reaching them?

Every successful business has customers. The challenge is to identify your specific target market, through some kind of analysis and study. In *Proverbs 19.2*, Solomon wrote: "It is not good for a person to be without knowledge, and he who makes haste with his feet makes a mistake."

- The reason for being specific, for really getting under the skin of your customers, is that in today's environment, quite good is never enough. You need to meet your customer and client needs EXACTLY, taking everything into account. And to do that, you need to know everything, to precisely define who they are, why they want you and what to do about it.

Gilbert Pagan

I. The CPA Story

Here's another story for you. A CPA specializing in tax returns moved into a small town of 2,000 people in the south, not currently being served by a tax accountant. There was no accountant in town and he believed that the entire 2,000 people, the entire market, could easily be his. All he had to do was move there, open an office, and he would be successful.

What he did not realize was that he did not have 2,000 potential customers. The average house had 3 people in it, so it was really about 650 potential customers. Furthermore, most of the people in this town filed their own returns because they were not complicated.

Of the 650 potential customers, only 175 used an outside service. Of those 175, a good portion of them used a low-cost tax service that charges about $75.00 for a return. Only 35 people would and could use a CPA to do their return. Evidently, this was not a big enough market for him.

If he had done an advanced review of the market, he would have realized that he would need customers from other towns to make his business viable. He was set up to fail from the start. This is why it's so important to remember to do some research and define your customer. The CPA did not conduct any basic research. I'm not saying you have to spend years doing this, but you should analyze the data and make a decision. You don't want analysis paralysis, and end up doing nothing. Entrepreneurs and visionaries make it happen.

- Take a good look at your business, sniff around. You should be able to identify many ways to identify your target market, while reducing your exposure and risk. From examining your figures to dealing with market needs by asking questions, research should be ongoing and constantly appraised.

- Each year, along with your usual tax returns and audits, make sure you audit the business personally. Take a good hard look at your clients and ask yourself how you can better serve them, get new ones and keep overhead low.

II. Your Image

In defining your customer, you need to choose your image. You need to determine in advance what your image will be for your business and then faithfully execute on the image. This starts the process in developing a reputation for your business.

Consistency in developing and offering good products is crucial when developing and sustaining a good reputation in the market place. *Proverbs 22:1* states, "A good name is more desirable than great riches; to be esteemed and respected is better than silver or gold."

In the old days, deals were done by handshakes and by the words that came out of your mouth. You could close a million dollar deal based on your word and reputation **without signing a document**. Imagine if you could open up a tab at a diner sit and eat, and not worry about having cash in your pocket. Your good name opened doors. Consistency in developing and offering good products is crucial when developing and sustaining a good reputation in the market place.

III. The Dollar Store Story

Let me give you an example about choosing the image you want to portray for your business.

Who likes to shop at dollar stores? Dollar stores need to offer low prices, as low prices are consistent with the dollar store image. The stores need to be neat, clean and very basic so customers can see that they are not paying for frills or fluff.

The next time you go to a dollar store, you will notice that they have every nook and cranny filed with merchandise. Why? Because they need to generate a lot of sales per square foot for the store space that they occupy which is usually in higher rent retail space that can generate a lot of foot traffic. You can also buy some stuff in bulk. They're all about selling all at low cost, generating a lot of traffic, and having simple space so you can find what you need and move on. That is the image; a low cost, efficient, no-frills service.

If you go to McDonalds, the image is hot, good, fast and relatively low cost food. You can pay $5.00 or so for a meal at McDonalds, and it is self-service. Go to a white tablecloth restaurant, and you will get table service, a bigger meal, and ambiance. Music, soft lights...I'm sure you get the picture—they are selling the experience.

- You need to decide which end of the market you will operate in. You will do this mostly by the prices you set and what you choose to sell. Public perception will take care of the rest. The idea is to operate where you are comfortable. If selling $1000 watches is your bag, then work in luxury retail. If you prefer shifting hundreds of crates of cheaper stuff, then you are better off in the wholesale arena.

Another example is Barnes and Noble. You can get a book, have a coffee, and sit there all day. They have set it up for people to stay there. In a used book store, you can get the same book for $5.00, whereas in B&N it could be $20.00.

- The right image in business is a combination of brand, graphical elements, public perception and your marketing materials. The final ingredient and arguably the most important, is you, the owner. Make sure you have the very best resources on hand here and ensure you personally represent the business at your very best. Everything from personal presentation, to your choice of clothes and even tone of voice will influence your image directly.

IV. Narrowing Your Market

Now that you have chosen your image, it's time to narrow your target market.

Let me give you an example. There was a builder that my company "Lease A Sales Rep" worked with, that was trying to grow his remodeling business. He initially tried to sell to everyone in the entire state—his motto was, "I will go anywhere in the state if they pay me enough." I would probably go too in the same situation, but in order to grow his business he needed to narrow his target market.

We worked together to have him focus on the areas that homeowners were getting remodeling done regularly. We pulled some building permit data and realized that many homeowners were doing room additions—about 2000 permits were pulled annually! So he did some initial research, which we discussed earlier is important, and realized that no contractor dominated the market in this area.

That's when he reframed his business as the "room addition guy", and if he could get 1% of the market, that would keep him and his team of sub contractors busy for 12 months.

If he had tried to hit the entire state with his service, he would have failed.

Always remember to narrow your market. Using a military analogy, be a sniper, don't use a shotgun. To do this in practice, think about specializing. Imagine being a mechanic; it would take years to become known as an expert. However, by specializing in just one particular niche–Japanese rare import carburetors– you could be known as an expert in no time.

- Think about taking your business and making it more specialized –geared for your most profitable customers. Select what is best, what earns you the most and really try to find the perfect way to deliver that product or service quickly. These days, the more specialized you are the better. The era of Jack of all Trades business is long over and people who dominate markets do so on very clearly defined terms.

- It is also important to trim the other way by getting rid of parts of the business which aren't working. Unprofitable clients, processes which are a major hassle for little return and anguishing waits should all be cut out. Business works both ways – you must increase profit and reduce cost. The sword has two edges.

Grow Your Business Using Biblical Principles™
V. Testing Your Market

The next point is about testing your market. In the book of *Job 12:11*, He states, "Does not the ear test the words it hears, and the mouth taste the food."

I tried some Lebanese food the other day, and I was a bit skeptical, but I took a small taste to see if I would like it, and then continued with an order and the meal.

The same goes for your business. Perform a small test to see the receptivity of the business. Place a small ad in the paper, get a few calls, talk to a few customers and get a feel for the need and price that customers will be willing to pay for your service.

- The market always knows best because the market is composed of customers. You should make every effort to use giveaways, free services, trials and surveys to see how the market likes what you are doing. Often, these will convert into sales and the exercise will make money where it began as a loss leader. Big supermarkets know this which is why you are often encouraged to try before you buy.

- Use all the tools at your disposal. Everything from free internet polls to popping samples through the mail can work. You can always simply grab a clipboard and pen and go out and ask questions. People appreciate businesses that cater to their precise needs and your work in researching and testing the market can be great public relations.

VI. *Offering a Great Service*

Offer a good service and overcome any resistance in yourself, your organization or your marketplace which lowers standards. The higher you aim with your business, the better your clients will perceive your worth.

Every business owner should strive to have the best possible service. You will need to define what you will deliver and then deliver that service with the best quality every time. Smart business owners know that it is not only the service, but it is the price that the market will bear that will also lead to business growth along with good service.

I know a butcher that opened a business in a low- to middle-income neighborhood. He offered high end meats, pork chops and chicken. The market he was targeting was very comfortable getting meat from the local supermarkets, and was not willing to pay a higher price for better cuts of meat and chicken.

However, he closed his shop, and reopened in a higher-end suburban community that was willing to pay more for better meats. So the right pricing was received in the right market.

- Quality takes many forms but the most important guide is value for money. If your customers recognize that you offer a great service or wonderful products, then you have won. If they feel short-changed, or overcharged or simply hard done by—you've done something wrong.

- Quality includes the speed of your service or delivery, the presentation of your business and your packaging, the way you communicate, what goes into your products, the costs and benefits and above all, your way of thinking and your attitude. You need to have quality at the forefront of every aspect of the business. It is a way of life for an enterprise and should become all-encompassing.

- Where there are gaps, they need to be filled quickly – there is an old saying that it takes years to build a reputation but seconds to lose it. This is proven day after day with scandals and recalls and bad publicity ruining well-known and previously solid businesses.

VII. Fixing the Price

1. Determining price:

In determining your price, you need to determine what the market will bear, and build your expenses and infrastructure around that price.

If you build a large retail hair salon with a lot of capital expenditures, store fixtures, expensive chairs, massage rooms etc, and the market will only pay $20.00 for a haircut, and your overhead is $6000 a month, that is a lot of haircuts just to break even.

Balancing all these factors is tricky, not in the least because none of them care about the other. Your clients don't worry that the rent is high; they want to pay the market rate. Equally, a landlord doesn't care what price you charge, he wants his rent each month and on time to boot.

- Most businesses learn pricing through trial and error and because market economics force them to get the balance at least partly right. There are some important constants however. The first is that it is easy to lower a price than raise it. Discounts and other special techniques aside, your base prices should be relatively constant. Anything sudden will disturb customers and cause a lot of head scratching and questions.

- For example, beginning with a low price which is unsustainable may lead to trouble when you are forced to raise it later. Will clients keep buying? Will they ask what the increase is for? Will they be concerned they have been lured in? By contrast, starting off with a high price and lowering it a little to please a customer is neither so dramatic it is suspect nor against the interest of the client as it is reducing.

- The trick of course is getting the right, higher price in the first place. The key here is selling quality and not price. With good quality and an exact match between need and desire and the product or service – the price is irrelevant. If you can't breathe and air is offered for $100 a bag, you'd buy it. Equally, if you could find the girl or man of your dreams, would you pay $10,000 just for the introduction?

- Surveying customers is also important because their perception is all important. As we know, a $5 packet of nuts is cheap at the North Pole but probably a little rich to a Chinese peanut farmer who has a ton in the backyard. Different customers perceive price at different levels. Moreover, price perception changes over time. A price considered "cheap" last year could be seen as wasted money the next. For example, a computer which cost $2000 in 1982 was a bargain, but try shifting one of those to a young enthusiast today with all our bargains!

Grow Your Business Using Biblical Principles™
VIII. Using Effective Advertising

1. Use advertising that works

In the book of *Amos 3:5*; it states "Does a bird fall into a trap on the ground when there is no bait in it? Does a trap spring up from the Earth when it captures nothing at all?" So the trap or bait you use to catch a bird is different than one for a rodent, or a bear. The same goes for advertising.

When you use advertising, set your goals as to how many sales or leads you want, then look at the investment amount needed to get to those sales or leads. If you have the capital to do that, then invest. If not, invest in advertising that will give you the best return for your money and in a form which lets you track the results.

Make sure that the ads you run in whatever media you choose for them are professionally made and make sense to the uneducated buyer. Make sure that you are consistent and repeat the ads. You need time for advertising to work. Figure out the method of advertising that works for you and stick with that method. Ask people where they heard about you and you will see a pattern that will confirm whether what you are doing is working or not.

Be very clear in communicating your message to your audience. *Isaiah 41:21* states "Present your case, the Lord says, bring forward your strong arguments, and make your case".

1. Who is and who should be your customer?
2. What advantage do you bring to the marketplace that will attract customers?
3. What image do you need in the marketplace? Dollar store? Or Saks 5th Avenue
4. Develop your 30 second pitch that outlines why someone should do business with you.

- Today, there are many media options for advertising that you could devote years into investigating them. As well as traditional media like newspapers and television, we now have internet streaming, clickable banners, websites, Facebook, Twitter, LinkedIn, SMS, mobile messages, picture messages – the list is endless.

- Also think about free ways to advertise. Word of mouth can get you a long way and the power of recommendations is incredible. Sending an email is free as well as many local calls where you could look for business. Other options include events where you could network, calling on shops or knocking on doors and also, using the Church.

- There are plenty of potential customers and helpers where you worship so seek them out. Don't be afraid to mix business with faith and even pleasure. There are countless opportunities to get the message across, even if you have to scrawl it on a napkin and personally deliver it.

Chapter Eight - Biblical Decision Making

This chapter will go a little deeper into "Biblical Decision Making". As believers, we are faced with decisions every day - whether it's deciding to take that job offer in another state, starting your own business because you can't find work and live your dream of being the man or gal instead of working for the man, or if it's deciding whether to let your kid go to college out of state, or live at home, or if they want to go to the military. With possible wars going on, should you let them?

Believers in particular have another avenue to get help with decisions, and that is through conversations with God. We often struggle with hearing God's voice; is the decision I'm making God's choice for me; is the Holy Spirit talking to me, is it the voice in my head that is telling me the decision I should be making? Determining what you are hearing, feeling, and sensing is often hard to do. Discernment is the key here. So many people make decisions without prayer; they lean on their own intellectual capacity, their ability to reason, look at the facts and make a decision, without God's input. Then they wonder why the decision did not work out.

Smart people seek counsel from others, pray about the decisions they have to make and are deliberate in trying to discern God's voice and plan for their lives. Remember that God's thoughts are not our thoughts, but the steps of a righteous man are guided by God because he talks to God. You can't get directions if you don't ask for them. I hate getting lost; I will pull over in a second and ask for directions. The same thing applies with God. Ask for directions in your decision making.

- We learned at first about the basic principles of Christian thinking, but Biblical Decision Making goes even further and forces us to examine every aspect of our personal and working lives. We are trying to compare ourselves with the very best, with God, and this should raise standards right across the board.

- In business it can often be easy to sit on the fence, to vacillate instead of being decisive and taking action. Biblical Decision Making means coming to a decision, making the call and then acting – all in accordance with the right principles.

- Take care to watch all sizes and shapes of decision. Small mistakes, tiny choices and little slips can be just as problematic as massive disasters. Things tend to grow, especially in a business which is going places so always keep a lookout for the small things as well as the more obvious.

- One of the biggest decisions of all is very subtle, and that is your decision about your attitude to the business. Are you really committed or are you just playing? Do your customers really come first? What are your real beliefs about the business?

- Finally, remember that decision making should often be collective. You need to involve customers, the wider marketplace and your staff and even your family in the things you do during the business day. The decisions have ramifications for everyone so open the discussion up and open your ears. It is often after balancing all the people who will be affected that you are able to come up with the solution to a difficult choice you are facing.

Grow Your Business Using Biblical Principles™

- For example, imagine a situation in which your price needs to change. The crops may have failed in some poor part of the world, or your supplier may have gone out of business. There could be many reasons but the important thing to note is that price can affect a lot of the people in your chain of thinking. Customers will react, your staff will react and will need to react to your customers, your bank manager may also react and at the end of the day – you will be reacting to what seems like a tiny change.

- Imagine what would happen in your cable television tripled in price, the ramifications would be far reaching. Would you cancel? Call up and complain? Lose patience? Stop watching? Would the cable company have more money for better programs? Or perhaps have less because people left due to pricing?

Chapter Nine – God's Authority Given to Man

In this chapter, I want to talk about God's authority given to man over his business and life. God has provided access to power and authority to all men that believe in Him. From Adam to Abraham, to Moses, to Jesus, all men that have consecrated themselves to God have chosen to live holy lives, treating others with respect through access to power and authority.

There is no power or authority without intimacy. Intimacy only comes through prayer and fasting. Prayer and fasting leads to the intimacy that leads to power. When you are in the presence of God through the intimate practices of prayer and the separation of yourselves through the sacrifice of fasting, the authority that you get comes naturally.

You have a sense of freedom when you come to God to ask for what you need: to move mountains in your favor, to cast out demons, health the sick, raise the dead. The authority that you carry if you are a man of God is amazing.

I. Using Authority in Your Business

Your message, your bearing, your whole brand should scream authority. Confidence and self-awareness of knowing things will turn out well is detectable by any potential client – and they love it. People prefer to do business with confident people; this is very logical. After all, would you buy an airline ticket from a nervous airline employee? Or cell phone service from a firm that admitted to being a bit shaky?

Business people need to learn to present a confident front. Being well prepared and having a great business concept is the keystone of maintaining a strong front. Build on this by developing sales skills, observing people and being generous, patient and peaceful with your contacts. Confidence can be learned and it grows the more you practice it.

II. The Power is Yours

"Dunamis" is the Greek word for power. Strength, ability, knowledge, skill – all these can give you power. Don't come and tell me that you have power and authority if you are not in church. Or you go to church once per month, show up late, or do not participate in the life of the church. You must be active in the church and use your fruits to benefit the church and others. This all ties into blessings, power and authority. Don't tell me that you think you have any authority when you are not using your gifts and power to help others. If you are a family man with kids and a wife, you have a different kind of authority over your wife and children. You need to have the power of protection, the authority of covering and the power to protect your kids from drugs, bad relationships and criminal activity.

If you are a business owner, you have power and authority over your business. Whatever is going on around you and whatever situations are facing other businesses does not apply to you if you are a believer. The rules are different; you have different tools at your discretion not available to others who are not in God's inner circle and who are intimate with Him.

It may help you to affirm your power through thoughts, words, and of course, deeds. By repeating and by expressing your power, it will grow. Many people use business mantras or affirmations each morning to power themselves up for the day. Even quiet affirmations through prayer and thought are powerful; it is the focus and the expression which is important.

III. Peter – The Number One Disciple

Let's talk about Peter, the #1 disciple. He is mentioned almost always as the first disciple when the disciples are mentioned. He is also considered the mouth piece of the disciples; he had a lot of power, but he was a man in conflict.

In *Matthew 14:23-30*, Peter walks on water.

"23 After Jesus he dismissed them, he went up on a mountainside by himself to pray. When evening came, he was there alone, 24 but the boat was already a considerable distance from land, buffeted by the waves because the wind was against it.
25 During the fourth watch of the night Jesus went out to them, walking on the lake.
The Jewish night is divided into four watches. The fourth or final watch is that time just before dawn, in the darkest hours.

Seek God in the early hours before the sun rise.

26 When the disciples saw him walking on the lake, they were terrified. "It's a ghost," they said, and cried out in fear.
27 But Jesus immediately said to them: "Take courage! It is I. Don't be afraid."
28 "Lord, if it's you," Peter replied, "tell me to come to you on the water."
29 "Come," he said. Then Peter got down out of the boat, walked on the water and came toward Jesus. 30 But when he saw the wind, he was afraid and, beginning to sink, cried out, "Lord, save me!"

His circumstances made him afraid, but that did not stop him from stepping out. He was the only one that stepped out of the boat.

Grow Your Business Using Biblical Principles™

Sometimes, you need to do something radical to see a different result. It's very easy to stay in the boat with everyone else and have a pity party. It is simple to do the same thing, to not look at the situation differently and end up hanging out with the wrong people. The negativity will rub off on you.

Peter was different; he thought, "I'm not going to die here, I am getting up and out of this situation, this storm, this crisis. I am taking the power and authority that God has given me to step out."

You may make that decision as a business owner to step out and change the game plan, but then a little wind or resistance comes your way and you want to run back to the boat, or stop altogether.

Peter started to sink after his eyes were off Jesus. Jesus was his strength and his authority; his source of power. He was plugged in when he had his eyes on Jesus. When he got unplugged, unfocused, he started to lose his authority and power. When he turned away his focus and gaze from God, he lost the confidence and subsequent power.

By the way, he was the only disciple that walked on water. He had doubts but he took a risk, He broke from the ranks, he did something different, he did not concern himself with what others would think. He was determined to change his circumstances.

The nay-sayers are not paying your rent, car payment, or home mortgage.

Peter was a man in conflict, a business owner in conflict, because after all he was a successful fisherman. Further in the bible you see that Peter would deny Jesus. He was a man in conflict. Even further along in the bible you will see that Peter was anointed and powerful.

I have realized that God often calls busy people to serve him and to serve others. Why? Because you have demonstrated already that you are a worker bee, a doer, not a pew warmer who sits back and gets fed all the time in the church but does not share some of the blessings that you have been given. So a few chapters down, In Matthew, Jesus gives Peter more power and authority.

Jesus said in *Matthew16:19, "You are Simon Peter." He identifies him by name, to get his attention, "Take your name and replace Peter and I will give you the keys of the Kingdom of Heaven. Whatever you lock on earth will be locked in heaven, and whatever you open on earth will be opened in heaven."

Lock and open implies a door - a door to a business, a door to a car, a door to an opportunity, a door to an introduction, a door to a divine appointment, a door to a divine connection, a door to spiritual and physical healing, a door to ………you fill in the blank.

Jesus has given all of us authority to lock and unlock doors in our lives. He says; "Whatever you lock on earth will be locked in heaven, and whatever you open on earth will be opened in heaven."

Peter was a man of authority and power given to him by God; he distributed authority, but also had individual authority. He was a man that wondered: what was all this God stuff; is this real? He was with Jesus, saw miracles, saw His power and still had doubts. He almost drowned in the water due to his doubts, he rejected Jesus three times before the centurions who were going to crucify Jesus. He stated, "I don't know him." He was a man in conflict and had his high days and down days, but he still had power and authority because he was still seeking God, was hungry for God and had intimacy with God.

Grow Your Business Using Biblical Principles™

IV. Here's something else to read about Peter:

Acts 5:12 *"The apostles performed many miraculous signs and wonders among the people. And all the believers used to meet together in Solomon's Colonnade. *[13]* No one else dared join them, even though they were highly regarded by the people. *[14]*Nevertheless, more and more men and women believed in the Lord and were added to their number. *[15]* As a result, people brought the sick into the streets and laid them on beds and mats so that at least Peter's shadow might fall on some of them as he passed by. *[16]* Crowds gathered also from the towns around Jerusalem, bringing their sick and those tormented by evil spirits, and all of them were healed."*

That kind of anointing, power and authority does not come unless you are intimate with God. God allows His power to flow through you. He healed people with his shadow.

In order to invoke power and authority over your business, you need to know what you are asking for. What doors do you need to open, and what keys do you need to open those doors with? What divine appointments do you need to get? Specifically, what are you seeking and targeting? In order to answer these questions, you need to have some sort of plan, roadmap, something that guides your path.

Chapter Ten – INC5000

In this chapter, I'm going to tell you how to grow your business into an INC5000 organization. Growing a business is very hard for many people. Customers are holding onto money, businesses are fearful of hiring because they don't know what the future holds. There is a slower economy—note that I say slower and not a "bad" economy—and this makes people nervous. They are confronted with their anxieties and they wonder what is going to happen.

My experience with these issues is to acknowledge them, confront them and move on. These issues that are happening around you don't necessarily need to affect you. In the book of *Psalms 91:7* we read, "A thousand may fall at your side, ten thousand at your right hand, but it will not come near you."

What that means is that companies like yours, competitors, or other businesses may fail, and they will close on your right and your left, but you will stay standing. If you remain steadfast, focused, pray, nose to the grindstone, make more calls, attend more events, advertise more, and work harder than everybody else-then you will survive.

Ignore the naysayers. Do what you have to do, and you will grow.

There are business owners today that place too much credence on what others say about their business, what they should and should not do to grow their business. While you may feel at times that you should try some "outside of the box" ideas, you end up not doing it. Quite often people will go with the crowd and do exactly what others in their industries try to do to grow their businesses. It's the fear that stops you from doing it. It's the fear of the unknown, and what people will think about your different or sometimes radical approach to marketing.

Tip # 1 – *Doing it Differently*

I believe in doing things differently. As an example, I like to use the power of video.

We believe in the power of video, because people are lazy and would rather watch a quick video about a product or service than read twenty pages of copy on a website.

But the vast majority of companies in my industry do not do video. That is precisely why I do it. If I listened to the complaints about expenses, or finding the equipment or the hassle, I would never have used new media in my business. But I didn't, I listened to my own voice and used my own research which told me, overwhelmingly, that video was the way forward.

If conventional wisdom and people tell us not to do something, more than likely that is when you have to do. Most people are not entrepreneurs. They don't think the way we do. Those who implement strategies that are different are entrepreneurs and set the path. Do what you need to do and develop you own journey. Many people provide you with feedback that runs counter-intuitive to what you want to do, because they are on their own journey, and will confuse their journey with yours.

The businesses that set the path and pave the way are those businesses that stick around. That is one of the strategies that we employed to grow our business into an INC5000 organization.

Remember the story of Zacchaeus the tax collector. We previously told his story, but it can also apply to the idea of using new and radical ideas to get progress.

If you remember, Zacchaeus was a tax collector in the book of. He wanted to see Jesus, but he was a short man, and the crowds were huge. So Zacchaeus, a very well dressed man, who had the equivalent of a 10,000 sq ft house, Armani suits and Mercedes Benz at that time, chose to do something radical for a man of his stature.

He ran ahead in his fine clothes, and climbed a tree. This is not something that most people would do at his social level. He was willing to humble himself, changed how he operated, in order to get what he needed—which was to see Jesus.

Take that approach with your business. Change it up, do something that others are not doing, even though you may feel uncomfortable doing it. Sometimes, we assume that we know all the angles in our business but on the contrary, we don't. If you have not tried another method to get customers, to generate leads, to build your business and you assume it will not work, but you have not tried it, then how can you reasonably state that it will not work? What experience have you based that on? Remember, ignore naysayers; they are not on your journey, they may confuse their journey with yours.

Tip # 2 – Widen Your Output

Grow your business with a multi-step strategy. Use e-mail, social media, direct mail, and calls. In these times, we have been bombarded with e-mails and social media and this has become a core practice of trying to grow sales for many organizations. I get them regularly. With the efficiency and cost effectiveness of it, many companies have come to rely solely on e-mail campaigns, or using Twitter and Facebook to generate sales.

My feedback on this is that e-mails supplement the sales process and can be used as a lead generation tool. Social media can assist

Grow Your Business Using Biblical Principles™

in building credibility with your potential prospects, and you may get a lead from social media alone, but you still need to employ a multi-touch strategy.

E-mail and social media are parts of a good strategy, along with direct mail, and some phone calls. Direct mail can include postcards or letters in collaboration with calls and e-mails, backed up with social media. We gave away some books and gift cards and that strategy definitely helped grow our business.

Jesus was the ultimate crowd-sourcer in the New Testament. Jesus had thousands of people following him, he would show up in a town, and thousands would be around him in a matter of hours. How do you think they communicated in those days? They did not have iPhones, Blackberry's, Internet, direct mail, Facebook or Twitter.

There is huge power in numbers and I will bet that there are at least ten new channels for marketing or ten little tweaks which would put you in front of a much bigger market than you ever dreamed. Make lists, do your research, talk to people and try to ensure for every angle you have another avenue to grow your business.

Tip # 3: Bang the Drum

Fill a room with your prospects. If you can get your ideal prospects together in a room to share what you do, or to give an educational session on a topic that is relevant to them, then you can potentially sell them on you, through you being the expert. You can follow up at some point in the future with a conversation on your product or service.

Remember that you need to tell as many people as possible that you exist. Then you need to tell the ones who are interested a little more, hook them slightly. Next, you go into more detail before finally closing deals with the smaller number who went all the way through the process. To do this right, you need a huge pool of original prospects.

Secondly, you need to share many positive and beneficial tips that infect your audience with a sense of urgency, excite them and make them feel like they need to know more. This comes through good story telling and excellent interpersonal skills.

Finally, get them together or go to their place, whatever it takes so you can use your personality and magnetism to close the deal. Being physically present is very important sometimes, so you will need to be prepared to put some serious mileage on your car and in time spent to make your business a success.

Tip # 4: Know Your Best Side

You have to determine what are you ruthless at? What I mean by ruthless is what are you the best at? When you do this, you are in your element, in the zone, it comes naturally - you flow. If you are a car mechanic, for example, you have the ability to hear a noise and know what the issue is with the vehicle. You enjoy working on cars and fixing them. You flow naturally. If you are a teacher, and you feel great joy when you are spreading knowledge, you flow naturally. If you are a marketing person, and you enjoy the strategy part of marketing, but not the execution part, then you flow in that gift. You flow with grace.

You have to identify what your best side is, and recognize that no one else is better than you in that area. You are the best. Many people have two or three areas where they excel, but when they cut to the core, they are really good at just one thing. You may be OK at Math, but you are an excellent writer. Do you see where I'm going with this?

Grow Your Business Using Biblical Principles™

Jesus was gifted in many areas, but He has an ability to speak in stories using parables to capture our attention, and educate us at the same time. He also has the skill to tell us a few things which might not be good or what we *wanted* to hear, but is what we *needed* to hear. He does this though parables, without you even realizing it. He was a good storyteller and crowd-sourcer.

Find your own specialty and use it to your advantage. This will help you to focus on your strengths, raise your confidence and also identify areas in which you might need help in.

Chapter Eleven – Increasing B2B Sales

The basics of business-to-business sales success are all related to handling customers with care to ensure their sales experience is the very best. Forget about price, because as the saying goes, price is quickly forgotten while quality is long remembered. It is a truism that while customers claim to be motivated solely by price, their real impulse to buy comes from the benefits of the product, the way they are managed and how much they need something that is offered.

B2B customers have more clearly defined needs than ordinary consumers. They can be more clearly targeted and approached through a greater variety of means. For the business owner, this allows a higher conversion rate of sales, because there is more to control, more to get *just* right. Conversion rates are vital to B2B sales and addressing conversion rates can get higher yields than simply increasing the number of prospects or by spending more on advertising.

Retaining clients has been proven to be vastly more financially advantageous than finding new ones. So once you have closed the deal, and a month after that, and next year, and if possible, forever – you need to keep your clients in the loop of your business.

One major consideration is that salespeople need to know the limits of their customers' patience. Customers don't enjoy a constant bombardment, and sales people must be sensitive as well as being perfectly knowledgeable of products and services that the company offers the market.

Grow Your Business Using Biblical Principles™

Customers buy benefits and need to know how your company will help them. A good salesperson should be able to explain this succinctly to the customer in a language they will recognize. This is because price, while important, isn't the biggest motivator which affects sales. The experience of the sale is more important than the numbers. This kills the big myth in business – price is not the be all and end all and businesses that are focused only on price soon go out of business. Service is the key.

Surveys have shown that there are two major problems with sales forces. The first is bad product knowledge and the second is too frequent contact with customers – hassling to get sales. That makes the second finding all the more important. Of the many habits that undermine the sales experience, these two are relatively easy to fix and accounted for 55 percent of the behavior customers described as "most destructive". These are easy fixes. More education on products and services, and to be "professionally persistent" but not overbearing will resolve these problems.

Fortunately, both damaging habits can be fixed. Companies can address a lack of product knowledge by centralizing content development to guarantee a uniform message and creation of compelling, value propositions for customers. And to ensure deep understanding, sales reps can receive training and on-the-job coaching, preferably side by side with the content-development team. Finally, sales reps don't need to know everything. When it comes to specifics, we found customers were more than happy to use self-serve or online tools and selectively tap specialist support for the most complex situations.

Striking the right balance between contacting customers too much and too little requires understanding their stated and actual needs. There should be a clear strategy for reaching out to customers based on needs and profit potential, with schedules dictating frequency.

The best contact calendars center around events that create value for customers, such as semi-annual business reviews, which provide an opportunity to assess customer needs and ensure satisfaction. The key is to recognize that customers are also looking to lower their interaction costs, so any contact with them must be meaningful.

The sales experience matters, and a good one starts by getting the basics right. Companies should examine exactly how they are performing by asking the following questions:

1. What are the most influential drivers of the sales experience?
2. What things are your sellers doing that could damage relationships?
3. How does the perception your customers have of your sales force compare to how they view your competitors?

It is only by knowing and understanding the answers to these questions that companies can begin to identify and pursue the right fixes and get more sales.

Chapter Twelve - Taking Risks

This chapter is all about risk taking. People under pressure are often afraid to take risks. The natural inclination is to become more conservative, more risk averse as our personal or business circumstances get tougher. But as any millionaire will tell you, this is not the way to get ahead. Businesses which profit do so by taking and managing risks.

At the writing of this book, we are coming out of a challenging economy. But there are many people still out of work. We have high unemployment, we have people knocking down the doors of food pantries, we have people living in apartments, trailers and houses with no heat, because they can only pay the rent or mortgage not the gas bill.

I know this because on a weekly basis, the social service arm of our business, "The Good Seed" along with the church, goes out and distributes food door to door in needy neighborhoods. We see the need every week. Many of these people are good people, but got caught in a bad situation where they lost their jobs. They placed their confidence in corporate America to provide for them, assuming there was job security. If someone who signs your check can tell you that you are being laid off, you have no control and hence no security. It's a false sense of security.

I. Keep a Clear Head

There are people who spend hours on the Internet and send in resumes to job postings along with thousands of others scouring the newspapers looking for work, when in reality, they may have the answer right in front of them but simply don't realize what that answer is. Because they are so focused on getting a job, they can't hear God talk or see possibilities because of the noise and the static. Those possibilities include starting your own business which involves taking a risk, as calculated as possible, but none the less a risk, and also entails being in control of your life,

Granted, starting a business is not for everybody; you have to do some soul searching, and this is not for the faint of heart. You need to do some heavy praying and fasting in order to determine when and if you should start your business. Jesus encourages business risk taking; that's right, it's in the Word and He provides encouragement for risk takers and blesses those who take risks.

Risks are taken by men and women that are not comfortable with the status quo. Of course, there are many unhappy people who settle for less because they are uncomfortable with change and won't take risk. Why? Change represents the unknown.

They have not seen the future, and feel that if change occurs, it might not be to their benefit. Business people take risk in proportion with what they believe will be the return. Simply put, the greater the risk, the higher the opportunity for profit.

II. Why Risk is Good

The simple answer to why risk is good is that the more risk your business absorbs and deals with professionally – the greater your revenues. The more investment of time, money and responsibility

Grow Your Business Using Biblical Principles™

you put in and the more you take risk from clients and manage it – the greater your worth in the marketplace.

The riskiest investments often have the biggest payouts. For example, an off shore oil company will invest large sums of money in exploration of petroleum-oil with say, 10 to 1 odds of finding oil. But the return is far greater than 10 to 1. Have you seen the gas prices recently? They are going up. The 10 to 1 return is risky but involves a hefty payout.

To hedge its bets, the oil company will drill many holes so their chance of success becomes greater. So although the majority of the wells will be dry holes, if they hit one hole with oil that will more than cover the cost of the other 9 holes or 100 holes they drilled.

With a 10 to 1 odd of not finding oil, but with a 15 to 1 return on investment if you hit oil, it seems that there is significant incentive to taking the risk.

III. Biblical Inspiration

The Bible encourages risk taking. Go to *Mathew 25-14:30*. Jesus uses this parable to teach us about risk taking. I will modify the interpretation in today's terms.

The Parable of the Thousand

[14] *"Again, it will be like a business owner going on a journey, who called his employees and entrusted his property to them. [15]To one he gave (talents) five thousand dollars[a], to another two thousand dollars, and to another, one thousand dollars, each according to his ability. Then he went on his journey. [16] The man who had received the five thousand dollars went at once and put his money to work and gained five thousand more. [17] Also, the one with the two thousand dollars gained two thousand more. They both*

doubled their money. ¹⁸ But the man who had received the one talent went off, dug a hole in the ground and hid his master's money. That would be the equivalent of a safe deposit box today.
¹⁹ "After a long time the business owner of those employees returned and settled accounts with them. ²⁰ The man who had received the five thousand dollars brought the other five thousand to the 'Business Owner,' he said, 'you entrusted me with five thousand. See, I have gained five thousand more.'
²¹ "His master replied, 'Well done, good and faithful servant! You have been faithful with a few things; I will put you in charge of many things. Come and share your master's happiness!'
²² "The man with the two thousand also came. 'Master,' he said, 'you entrusted me with two thousand; see, I have gained two more.'
²³ "His master replied, 'Well done, good and faithful servant! You have been faithful with a few things; I will put you in charge of many things. Come and share your master's happiness!'
²⁴ "Then the man who had received the one talent came. 'Master,' he said, 'I knew that you are a hard man, harvesting where you have not sown and gathering where you have not scattered seed. ²⁵ So I was afraid and went out and hid your talent in the ground. See, here is what belongs to you.'
²⁶ "His master replied, 'You wicked, lazy servant! So you knew that I harvest where I have not sown and gather where I have not scattered seed? ²⁷ Well then, you should have put my money on deposit with the bankers, so that when I returned I would have received it back with interest.
²⁸ " 'He took the talent from him and gave it to the one who has the ten thousand. ²⁹ For everyone who has will be given more, and he will have an abundance. Whoever does not have, even what he has will be taken from him. ³⁰ And throw that worthless servant outside, into the darkness, where there will be weeping and gnashing of teeth.'"

In this example the employee, who took the money and did nothing lost any opportunity for profit. Hence his master scolded him for being irresponsible.

- As Jesus teaches, we should not shy away from opportunity or the risk that accompanies it. This is very important because for most people, risk signals danger. They have a visceral reaction to risk, whether it is financial, physical or an intellectual challenge. Conquering this reaction is important for anyone with a business. A calm acceptance of risk and an ability to channel risk somewhere safe is what usually separates a successful business from the failures.

IV. Babe Ruth & Thomas Edison

I would like to make a baseball analogy. Babe Ruth the Yankees Baseball player was the home run king before Hank Aaron broke his record. Then Barry Bonds broke Hank Aaron's record.

Babe Ruth in that time hit 714 home runs, but he struck out 1330 times. He would always swing for the fences, but he got to break a record by swinging. Everyone remembers Babe Ruth's home run record and not the strike outs.

Thomas Edison failed 25,000 times in his attempt to make a battery that would store power. According to Thomas Edison, he did not fail, but learned 25,000 different ways not to make a battery.

Everyone remembers Thomas Edison's successes and his inventions like the light bulb, and not his failures. Thomas Edison has the most patents at the US patents office with 1093 in total, and many inventions to his credit.

The Lord measures how many times we get up, not how many times we fall. The challenge in risk taking for many is the actual fear of failure and what people will think of you - your family, friends, business associates, whomever.

- For business owners, there must always be the will to keep going no matter what. All business involves risk, and for those without an established operation, there may be hardships and setbacks. As the financial crisis has shown, no-one is immune from being taken down a peg or two, so keep at it.

V. Risk Aversion

As a business advisor once told me about my risk aversion, "Don't worry about those around you. They aren't paying your rent, mortgage, putting food on the table. Do what you've got to do, because later on, no one will remember it when you are wildly, unimaginably successful."

Always remain humble to the fact that God was there to pick you up, and help dust you off for the next challenge. I want to share with you this passage from *2 Timothy 4-7-8.*

"[7] I have fought the good fight, I have finished the race, I have kept the faith. [8] Now there is in store for me the crown of righteousness, which the Lord, the righteous Judge, will award to me on that day—and not only to me, but also to all who have longed for his appearing."

- There is a reward at the end and a silver lining inside every cloud. But you have to break through the pain barrier, become used to risk and take a leap of faith to grow your business.

Chapter Thirteen - 3 Steps to Grow Your Business

In this chapter, I want to talk with you about the 3 steps to business growth if you are a Christian business owner. If you implement these steps you will see a positive change in your business. We will tie these steps into the Word; I'm going to put my seminary and business education to work for you.

These steps can apply to those in business, and those thinking about starting one as they are spiritual steps, independent of our circumstances in the commercial world.

Step 1: Pray and Fast

I have spoken to many business owners and people who want to start businesses and their prayer life is either non-existent, meaning they don't have one, or they only pray in Church on Sundays.

1.2 Chronicles 7:14 *"if my people, who are called by my name, will humble themselves and pray and seek my face and turn from their wicked ways, then will I hear from heaven and will forgive their sin and will heal their land."*

In order to get some kind of direction, inclination in your spirit, or to get a confirmation on something that you need to do for your business, or an idea that you want to implement to start a business - you need to pray.

In today's society, people want everything fast. They seek counsel from people that may have good business sense, but are not believers. You *can* get good counsel from someone who is not a

Christian, but if you are a Christian, you need to watch the type of counsel that you are getting, because you aren't like everybody else. Your life has more purpose, your life has more direction, your steps are guided and your connections are Divine in nature. You need to watch who gives you counsel.

- Deep thought and prayer are essential in the fast paced, frantic business world. With time to reflect and to think issues through, you will be able to make the right choices without being forced into situations you don't like.

Many believers that I know are saved Christians, whose church life or servant life are based on working in the church and serving others. But they may not be totally plugged into God, but are going through the motions. They are very analytical, read a lot of books, and go to a lot of seminars. These things are not bad in themselves, but they need to be coupled with a solid, strong, purposeful, and consistent prayer life.

You can't get all your answers from books and non-believers.

You need to be plugged into God and our communication system with God is not through web chat, Blackberry, Facebook or Twitter, it is through prayer. It's by putting your head on the ground, and praying to God and telling him, "I'm not getting up from this floor until you tell me what I have to do!" That is the praying part.

The fasting part is hard for many people. I love to eat; my wife and I really enjoy Italian food and a real breakfast for me is 2 eggs sunny side up, with greasy home fries, bacon, and some toast.

To fast is to sacrifice. Jesus fasted and prayed for 40 days. All you need to do is fast for a few hours in the morning; just drink some liquids, pray, do your normal work, but be mindful that when you fast and pray that you have a purpose.

- Keeping a regular schedule and making sure you stick to it are crucial. Remember that a single, constant drop of water will wear down any stone and have the best possible, effective business habits. Almost any problem in the marketplace can be reduced gradually and safely as long as you give it enough attention.

So today, this morning, like every morning, I will be fasting and praying till 12pm. I will not eat any solid food, only juice or water, and pray before I head out to the office or work. I will read a scripture or two at the office. I will be purposeful as to what I am fasting and praying about. Let's say I want growth in my business, I want 20 new customers that will pay me $100,000 dollars over the course of the next 6 months. Be purposeful and identify your specific needs.

I know that this may sound radical to some, but to get extraordinary results you need to implement extraordinary measures.

Step 2: Ask in the Name of Jesus

Let's go to *John 14:12-14* (New International Version)
"[12] I tell you the truth, anyone who has faith in me will do what I have been doing. He will do even greater things than these, because I am going to the Father. [13] And I will do whatever you ask in my name, so that the Son may bring glory to the Father. [14] You may ask me for anything in my name, and I will do it."

When you ask in the name of Jesus, wild things happen. That is because the forces that impede you, the mountains that block you, the rocks that are thrown at you, the chains that can be cast upon you in respect to your business, your dreams, and your vision, all fall at the name of Jesus.

Demons tremble when they hear that name. When Jesus died, he sacrificed his life so that we may have life, and also access the Kingdom and the power. When you invoke the name of Jesus, you invoke the power of His blood that was shed. There is power in the blood.

- Always be explicit and ask for what you need. Ask questions, search for facts and evidence. Ask for success, ask to find the right clients, and above all, ask for the deal to be yours.

I'm going Theological now. The name of Jesus invokes the power of His Blood to spread over every aspect of your life, and that includes your business, your desire to be in business, your dreams and your family as well. And in this scripture, Jesus repeats a verse twice to ensure that it gets through to you. And it's done for emphasis, and to share that it has power.

Here is an example of a prayer:

"Jesus, cover every single aspect of my life with your blood. I ask for everything I need in your name. Your word says ask in the name of Jesus and it will be given to me. So I am asking."

God likes when you use His word in communicating with him. He realizes that His child knows His word and makes Him say, "I have to respond and do something."

Grow Your Business Using Biblical Principles™

Step 3: Tithe

We are going into a controversial area. When you start talking to people about giving money to the church and to God people can become really nervous! This is a very common reaction.

I have met so many people in my Christian walk that are waiting for God's blessing, but have not seen the financial blessing because they have chosen not to tithe. Or they give to some causes sporadically, not the church, where they get fed, and are loved. The keys to financial prosperity and success are secured in part through tithing, service, and holiness.

Let's read Malachi 3:8-10.
"Will a man rob God? Yet you rob me. But you ask, 'How do we rob you?' In tithes and offerings. ^{9} You are under a curse—the whole nation of you—because you are robbing me. ^{10} Bring the whole tithe into the storehouse, that there may be food in my house. 'Test me in this,' says the LORD Almighty, 'and see if I will not throw open the floodgates of heaven and pour out so much blessing that you will not have room enough for it. ^{11} I will prevent pests from devouring your crops, and the vines in your fields will not cast their fruit,' says the LORD Almighty. ^{12} "Then all the nations will call you blessed, for yours will be a delightful land," says the LORD Almighty."

A tithe means 10%. If you come home with $100 a week, you give to God 10% ($10.00). If you are a member of a church, then you give it there first. If you want to give more, do so, or to other causes, but the tithe should be brought into the store house, the church, so that there may be food, meaning the word can be preached, and souls can be saved.

"Test me, test me. In this, and I will throw open the flood gates of heaven"

- The tithe is an expression of your will to give before you receive. In business, you need to put out a lot of energy and often expenditure before you can see returns. Be generous and don't give up – often, it takes time for relationships to cement and sales to flow.

Be prepared to give to God faithfully over time. This is a marathon, not a race. God needs to see your commitment, your heart, and wants to see that you are faithful. Then He will move on your behalf. Be patient.

Grow Your Business Using Biblical Principles™

Chapter Fourteen - Jesus Speaks to the Masses

This chapter is all about how Jesus spoke to the masses with his unique style, preaching to thousands at a time when social media and even newspapers did not exist. The same techniques Jesus used can inspire you to communicate with your market and your connections.

I. Introduction

How did Jesus communicate? He told stories to pull people in called "parables". He was a great story teller, with twists and turns that kept people engaged. He was so good that He was able to pull in thousands of people for the Sermon on the Mount, 5000 for the massive feeding and miraculous multiplication of the fish and bread. He did this all without social media, TV, radio, cell phones or Facebook!

- The key technique, if you haven't guessed already – is using storytelling. It is often no use just explaining facts, or numbers, or worst of all - prices. For people to understand your message, and for them to sell themselves your offerings, the best medium you have is the story. Story format is universally understood and forms part of human nature. Good sales and marketing techniques utilize stories to put businesses in the right context for consumers.

When people heard that Jesus was in town, the methods that the town folk used to inform the masses that he was there included horns, bells, smoke signals and pounding of drums through the mountains that formed echo chambers. This told the population that someone of importance was in town.

- Note that you need to make announcements, let the world know there is something of importance to be said about your company. Never be afraid to bang your own drum in your business and make sure before you even begin talking about benefits or sales proposals that you have informed everyone of your abilities and that you are in town.

Communications can never be more effective than their source. Jesus communicated in such a way that people were amazed at His authority, power and truthful insights. The problem with so many communicators in our modern world is that they rely on theories that have not been given to them by God. Let us look at some of the principles of communications that Jesus demonstrated to his disciples that continue to stand the test of time:

II. Jesus' Methods: Befriending and Relationships

It is helpful to observe Jesus' methods. We can clearly see several key aspects to his ministry: addressing needs and really using the principles of building relationships. When we meet people face-to-face we can connect with them intimately, sit with them, eat at times and communicate in a meaningful way. This creates a sense of community which is crucial to any business. We must also learn how non-Christians think and how Jesus communicated with people who had yet to adopt his ideology.

Imagine for a moment that a person is living in the culture of Jesus' day. World history doesn't arrive via digital signals to screens in living rooms or Blackberries or iPhones. Books were not generally available, and you couldn't listen to your favorite speakers via tapes or CDs. Everything was verbal, or scratched onto papyrus or into wax.

Grow Your Business Using Biblical Principles™

How then did Jesus mass communicate, and what do his ancient methods have to say about our future spiritual life? How did he pass on his values and equip twelve men to start a church that would shape civilizations and attract billions of followers?

Making friends and building relationships wherever we find them is the key to forming a successful Christian business. Without judging, we need to connect with all those around us. Your customers and prospects should first become friends, and then over time convert them into deals. All good salespeople know that the first priority in a meeting is making a friend.

III. The Nature of Communication

By definition, communication is an impartation of living ideas, evoking mental and emotional responses. It involves hearing, understanding, encountering, listening, and responding as well as speaking and delivering. The ideal communication happens when the true meaning and intended aim of the communication is accurately transmitted to the receivers.

The process of Jesus' communication involved encoding and putting the message into understandable language. It involved decoding, as his audience interpreted the message contextually. He defined his perception of the message, associating his perception with known information, interpreting his message in the light of previous knowledge. He then formulated the message into ideas, verbalizing the message into words, transmitted the message and received feedback both verbally and nonverbally from his message.

You can follow the same pattern in your business life. First, get your message clear and easily understood. Next, explain to the prospects and customers everything they need to know. Relate your business to things they know and give them ideas for improving their lives with your products and services. Finally, ask for the deal, ask for a commitment and then communicate with them over time to improve things for both of you and the likelihood of a sale.

IV. Christ's Principles of Communications

1. First, to become better communicators, we must learn to become good listeners. *"Everyone should be quick to listen"*.

2. Second, to become good communicators, we must learn to become guided speakers. *"... slow to speak ..."*

3. Finally, to become good communicators, we must learn to become gentle responders. *"... slow to become angry."*

It's tempting to think Jesus succeeded because he was a great orator. He clearly was gifted. He sat in a boat and using the acoustic properties of the nearby coastline, spoke to thousands. He taught more than four thousand people for three days on another occasion.

As you read the Biblical record, you will find few long speeches or lengthy sermons. The Sermon on the Mount narratives don't take much more than seven minutes to read out loud, so Jesus must have been doing something else other than wearing his audience down verbally. If we are to follow Jesus and create counter-cultural communities, we are clearly going to have to do more than ensure that our Sunday services are finished by an eloquent forty-minute sermon, useful as that may be.

- Keep your message tight and use the minimum number of words. Jesus knew how to communicate concisely and without confusing his audience. You should learn how to edit your long speeches and lengthy correspondence down to the bare minimum.

When Jesus spoke to or ate with people deemed unworthy by others, he sent out powerful signals. Mundane behavior such as eating together spoke of acceptance, acceptance sparked trust, trust released hope, and hope sought salvation. Most times, we often start our contact with the non-Christian with verbal declarations of our faith. Offers of healing prayer may come next. Eventually, they may share the everyday normality of a meal with us before we ask God to bring peace to their home and family.

- Learn to speak to people on their own terms, using their customs and their culture or just basic human good principles. They will understand your message better if you put it to them in their way.

Jesus' words to his disciples as he sends them out to prepare the way for him are instructive. Consider the order in Luke 10:5-9. *"Whatever house you enter, first say, 'peace to this house!' and if anyone is there who shares in peace, your peace will rest on that person; but if not, it will return to you. Remain in the same house, eating and drinking whatever they provide, for the laborer deserves to be paid. Do not move about from house to house. Whenever you enter a town and its people welcome you, eat what is set before you; cure the sick who are there, and say to them, 'the kingdom of God has come near to you."* Part of the challenge of this passage lies in the order in which Jesus suggests things be done.

In the business context, Jesus was a relationship-builder. He tried very hard to connect with people. By connecting with people, he was able to bring their guard down, share his message of salvation and close the sale. This is exactly what needs to happen in the business world. We connect with people, their guard comes down, we share our message, and we then do business together. Jesus did it with a lot of grace and love, and in the context of business we need to do the same. We do this by identifying the need of the customer or prospect and try to meet that need and close the deal.

V. Declare Peace

This formed part of a common greeting at the time. But it could be much more than a mere verbal punctuation mark. Does it provoke us about our tendency to pray "against" things when we begin to think about how to pray for our area, town, or street? Jesus is inviting us to invite him to bring peace to that area. The mere announcement that God's peace is coming to that place is a form of spiritual warfare that drives away destructive forces that may have strongholds there.

- Come to work with a good heart. Your business should be a place of peace where things run smoothly.

VI. Eat with People

Eating together allowed discussion, signified acceptance, and was a redemptive act in its own right when practiced by Jesus with the social outcasts of the day. It reminds us to be with people in the ordinary rhythms of their lives, building friendship and trust.

- In business terms, try not to separate your clients' lives from their businesses, and adapt to their timings and lifestyle.

VII. Take as Well as Give

Creating strong friendships depends on mutual care. It's OK for us to lean on our friends who have not gone to churches. Jesus asked the Samaritan woman for a drink. He then gave her living water!

- Business should be a win-win situation every time you do a deal. You AND the client or customer should benefit. Also, remember that to get new business, you might need to do a few favors or help out to get your name out there. As you give, so shall you receive…

VIII. Pray for their Healing

Jesus prayed for people to be healed. Some were deeply grateful and no doubt became part of his band of followers. Others, including nine lepers, expressed little thanks. In our culture, people seem ready to be prayed for, even though not all acknowledge the healer who might come to their aid. Healing prayer seemed to be a gateway for the message of Christ's life; it enabled trust to grow, and readied people to hear the message of the Kingdom.

- Take time to think about your customers and your business and pray for the needs of the people in and around it. Self-reflection can yield many answers and a kind prayer for them will never go unanswered.

IX. *Declare the Kingdom*

This next story is about a Hindu Kharga festival in Bangalore. The people sweltered in the sun as they waited for the doors to the temple open. At one end of the street, a church group held up banners proclaiming that God hated idol worship. Further down the street another church group, noting the plight of the queue, made gallons of cold drinks and offered them to people as they waited. Hundreds of young adults had some of their caricatures of Christians – encouraged by the banner wavers – undone by a simple act of acceptance and help. A church group declared peace to the crowd and helped feed them. This group likely got the opportunity to pray for their needs and declare the good news of Jesus' kingdom.

- Be sympathetic to your clients and know your market's needs. This church group was able to reach the hearts of the Hindus by being generous and understanding, where others were more concerned with fostering stereotypes.

Jesus didn't send out his followers alone. They ventured into the wider world together. Jesus often met with those considered "sinners and publicans" in the company of several of his followers. We will not want to face some of the challenges of the culture we live in alone, but we will never change it by hiding in our castles and staging confrontational raids on the hearts of the lost via occasional street preaching or door knocking.

- Get out there. Don't be afraid to travel and mix to get your message out to the people who need to hear it. Your business needs a global perspective.

In various towns and cities around the world, door knocking is starting to work again because its primary purpose is not to engineer a conversation but to basically make contact, offer prayer, or convey information about church events or children's clubs. At first, one is given seconds at the door, but in time trust is built; people become our acquaintances and then our friends.

- Keep it personal. Don't be seduced by ideas of connecting purely with technology or remotely. Get into people's homes and onto their doorsteps.

As we consider matters of social justice, are we motivated by pity or compassion? Pity says, "I will help you because I feel guilty, or maybe because I feel superior." Compassion says, "I will help you because you're human, made in the image of God and worthy of dignity, friendship, and aid." Jesus was color-blind, status-blind, and gender-blind. He didn't see the divisions we often see. He created a church where there is neither Jew nor Greek, male nor female, slave nor free.

- Don't be prejudiced, and treat all your clients with equal grace. Often, preconceptions are wrong and will lead to situations in which you could have sold more or made more profit had you simply opened your eyes without prejudice.

X. Summary

1. Jesus wanted his disciples to be transformed in their thinking before they could qualify to communicate his truth to others. Jesus said, "A good tree will produce good fruit." The Lord knew that without the willingness to be cleansed, empowered and instructed by the Holy Spirit, no one could do the works of God using just their own human wisdom. Communicating the truth of God can only be done through an understanding of the scriptures. Visions, dreams and spiritual experiences are no substitute for the way that God's word can transform the perspectives of an individual. Jesus wants every believer to take the advice from Paul who wrote, *"Do your best to present yourself to God as one approved, a workman who does not*

need to be ashamed and who correctly handles the word of truth." (2 Timothy. 2:15) Without a disciplined study of the scriptures, we lack a solid foundation from which to communicate truth.

2. Jesus knew that communication of truth is done through interpersonal involvement, relationship building, and group ministry experiences. On many occasions, the disciples of Jesus learned a great deal of truth by working alongside the Lord in real ministry situations. If you want to learn how to communicate, be willing to be 100% involved in ministries with other Godly people. (Matthew 4:19) The disciples learned by following the example of the great communicator.

3. Jesus involved as many senses of his audiences as possible to enhance communication. When Jesus fed the 5,000 he actively involved people's sense of touch, taste, sight, hearing and smelling. The Lord knew that good communications would involve multiple channels working simultaneously. When we are able to engage our audiences in as many senses as possible for the maximum time, our communications will have a long lasting impression.

4. Jesus considered each person's perspective so he could adjust his message according to every situation. The Lord crafted each message to suit the greatest needs of the person or audiences he addressed. When he gave the Sermon on the Mount he addressed the problems of poverty, depression, persecution, misunderstanding, purpose, and many everyday problems. Communicating in a way that addresses the emotional, mental, social, cultural, economic, family and spiritual problems of ordinary people is the most powerful form of human contact. Speak to broken hearts that are really hungering and thirsting for answers to life's problems.

Grow Your Business Using Biblical Principles™

5. Jesus communicated in a way that tried to remove as many distracting barriers as possible. Most people have natural filters - prejudices, wrong assumptions, bitterness, etc. in their brain to screen out messages that may at one time have given them personal pain. The Lord tried to assure people of his love before speaking truth. Jesus helped everyone feel that he did not condemn or hold any prejudice. The Lord did not see any reason why they could not get their problem solved. People were not only inspired by Christ's communication, but they were instructed and persuaded to follow after truth. Jesus was the master of doing impossible things that no one else could do. People knew that Christ's truth could work in ways that we may not be able understand, but it was still worth believing.

6. Jesus used credible mediators in the culture to enhance his communications. When Jesus went to various parts of society his disciples represented a wide variety of professions, social classes and educational levels that reinforced his credibility. Good communications often need contextual witnesses to enhance veracity, reliability and suitability. When people saw the changes that Christ's truth had brought about in the lives of the disciples, they were more apt to believe because of his use of credible mediators.

7. Jesus made great efforts to balance the emotional, rational, inspiring, behavioral and spiritual aspects of every message. Without a holistic approach, our communications can often come across as deficient and lacking in breadth. For example, one day, the Lord sent the disciples out to preach. As they went, he gave them authority and power to drive out all demons and cure diseases and to preach the kingdom of God and to heal the sick. (Luke 9:1,2) When they returned, the disciples declared, *"Lord, even the demons submit to us in your name."* Christ said, *"Do not rejoice that the spirits submit to you, but rejoice that your names are written in heaven."*

Chapter Fifteen – How to Get More Leads

This chapter is all about leads: how to get more leads, get your voicemails returned, and get that appointment with your ideal customer. A lead is any contact that may become a sale, or translate into some new business. A lead could come from a potential client picking up the phone, or you might be digging leads out by phoning prospects or doing a little community networking. However you find them, without leads there can be no sales.

Your thoughts about how you currently run the sales and marketing aspect of your business will be challenged in this chapter. If you feel some sense of discomfort in what you are reading, this section has particular relevance for you. I speak with so many business owners and large enterprises that are having difficulty in getting leads, meeting with people and getting their voicemails returned. Many people who are otherwise very effective in managing their businesses fall down when they apply their talents to drumming up new business.

Some of the large clients we serve, like Hewlett-Packard and Dell have challenges getting sales. Not because they don't have good products, but because prospects are doing a lot more with less, they are busy, unfocused, and would love to talk "if only the day had 35 hours in it." Even the big fish with all their resources find sourcing new customers tough. Large businesses have different challenges than smaller business. They can't move as quickly, and are slower to make decisions. Smaller enterprises have an advantage and that is speed. Bear that in mind when competing with larger companies.

Grow Your Business Using Biblical Principles™

Several common factors are at work here. First and foremost, there is a psychological block in many business people when it comes to sales and marketing. Unless you have a background in publicity or closing deals, the process can seem intimidating and filled with social embarrassment. Some people are resistant to the idea of using sales techniques and lead generation strategies because they themselves don't like being sold to. Others are nervous about meeting large numbers of people in order to find potential clients, and are more used to long term established relationship building.

The other important factor is that businesses are getting more and more competitive while customers are getting more and more demanding and cynical about the sales process. Not only are other competitors constantly attracting and trying to close your potential prospect, but the potential customers themselves make things difficult because of the scale of their demands and their experience with sales people and the sales process. They know that if they push hard enough, or hold out long enough, they may get a better deal.

So how do you get more leads, more appointments and get your calls returned? To succeed in the leads game, a business owner needs dedication to handle the volume of work required, skill to differentiate himself or herself from the competition and persistence to handle the many knocks which arise. There are also a range of techniques which you can focus on to break the process down into manageable steps:

Step 1 – Know Thy Customer

Knowing all about your customers, their needs, their world and their beliefs is the best way to begin any kind of sales operation. After all, without knowing what they like and what they want, how will you sell the right product or service to the right customer?

Ask as many questions as you can. Knowing thy customer means investigating, interviewing and researching to discover the truth. Ask questions both of the business and of the customers themselves. Things you need to know include:

- Who is your ideal customer? Why do they suit your business? Is it just a question of profit or are their other things which make this type of customer especially valuable?

- What can a customer afford to spend on your product or service? How does this compare to your competitors? Where will they find the money? Does offering financing or flexible payments help you to help customers and turn over more sales?

- Where are they? Does their home or workplace location influence things like delivery or communication with your business? Do customers buy from further afield or from abroad? Are there other countries or states you could find customers in?

- Why might they want your product? Is their reason for possibly using your company based on a need, based on enjoyment or a question of speed or convenience? What would their ideal product or service comprise?

- Will they talk to you? How can you get in touch with potential customers? What method of communication will give you the highest response rate? Why might customers be reluctant to talk? Will they discuss other products or competitors?

- Are customers aware of your firm? What other firms are helping them or are in a business relationship with them?

- Are your customers private individuals, companies, governments or all three? How many employees do they have? What are their annual revenues? Who is on the board? Who makes purchasing decisions?

The more you know, the more you can tailor what you offer and how you choose to say it. Valuable information always arises from this kind of questioning, and often forms a vital part of business and operations plans.

Step 2 – Go Out And Seek

In this step, we want to make sure you and your associates are looking in the right places and are out and about raising your profile. You need to be in the right place at the right time to get good leads, so make an assessment of where your potential leads might be:

- Conferences & shows for the public.
- Business journal subscribers.
- Business leader breakfasts.
- Seminars & industry events.
- Online or using social media.

- Associations.
- Socializing or accessible within the community.
- Networking.
- Educational seminars.

Also assess where you and the business are physically in relation to others:

- Where are you hanging out and where have you located your head office or staff members?
- Is your social and business environment conducive to meeting new clients?
- Where are you networking and are you making the most of your opportunities?
- Who have you met recently who might help? Have you mentioned your business and how did you present it?

You should also look at things geographically:

- What states or regions are my best leads going to be in?
- What about the rest of the world?
- Do they all speak English?

The idea is to find the leads, and then get yourself in front of them. Remember, you can find leads everywhere: close to home, within your circle and anywhere there are people who might need your product or service. Think both locally and globally and don't be afraid to try new potential markets. Be persistent and you will turn up many potential leads in less time than you might think by focusing your efforts in the right places.

Grow Your Business Using Biblical Principles™
Step 3 – Talk to Them

Once you've found a stack of potential contacts, it is time to make a connection with them. Approaching new people might seem intimidating but it can be easy with a solid plan and a little preparation.

- First, set some targets. For example, at networking events you could agree to meet 4-5 people, for business or strategic partnerships and set another target to setup another 3 follow-up meetings or calls. For combing through long lists of potential contacts, you could set a target of 100 emails or 10 new additions to your mailing list each week. Targets keep reasonable limits on your work and give you ways to measure your performance. They are also important as they keep your mind on the bigger picture and don't place too much emphasis on the inevitable individual leads which go bad. Targets keep you moving.

- Second, prepare well to be memorable. The two secrets here are asking great questions and having a few well-practiced lines which bring out the best in you. These techniques are designed to build a quick rapport with your contacts and lend a very personal touch to all your efforts. So, be curious about your leads; ask them what they like to do for fun; ask them where they came from, what their story is. You need to know all these little details to tailor your approach and to personalize things like benefits and establish needs. Give them something to help them connect with you. Try talking about movie scenes or music, or anything which bridges the gap and establishes your unique identity.

- Third, revise your pitch and refine it for every particular lead. In the end, after establishing contact and then building rapport, you need to talk about how your business could help this new contact. This is why you must have your materials, a good sound bite or two and relevant examples at hand to help you pitch your proposal. You might want to do this verbally, in which case, practicing with a tape recorder or your partner is useful, or else in writing, in which case you need to thoroughly polish your written marketing material.

In working up to your pitch, there is no need to rush things. You can be gentle, but you must be focused on finding new opportunities and actually turning them into sales. This means finding out how you can help and then explaining your proposal clearly and finally asking for the deal. You need an answer to either move onto another lead or deal with a new sale, so be subtle but keep your eye on the time you expend on each prospect. Some people may be afraid of this shift into a business territory and then an attempt to close a deal, and it is vital to have confidence and enough professionalism to realize this can never be a solely social endeavor. Practice makes perfect with communications and you can learn from every contact you talk to. Most people find this reluctance declines over time and their conversion rate of prospects grows. So ask for the sale. You don't get, if you don't ask.

Step 4 – Connecting Electronically

There are so many opportunities today for making new connections thanks to the Internet and a raft of new technologies. Indeed, this area is so important it is worth a separate, distinct step in your process. Electronic communications make finding pools of

Grow Your Business Using Biblical Principles™

leads and getting them involved in your ideas is cheaper, faster and easier than ever before.

You'll already know many of these suggestions, but here are some possibilities for finding leads and making contact using the latest technology:

- Using social media like Facebook, Twitter or LinkedIn to find followers and interact with customers directly.

- Using sites like Twitter to send concise messages and marketing to large numbers of potential clients.

- Using email or e-cards to send messages which provoke a response or raise questions in your prospects' minds.

- Using text messaging to stay in touch with clients who rely on their mobile phones and who may be roaming over a wide area.

- Using search engines like Google to find contacts and to advertise using search engine optimization and pay per click campaigns.

- Using Skype to video conference with a bunch of potential clients and ask them about how you could tailor the perfect service or product for them.

- Use Go To Meeting to create and launch webinars.

Approaching leads always involves finding, contacting and then managing responses with a group of potential leads, moving further along the sales process with each contact.

For example, here is how an approach might go that weaves electronic communication into conventional marketing and a highly personalized approach:

1) Connect on LinkedIn and send a quick note to get some attention.
2) Write a note on LinkedIn and get a physical address.
3) Send a card with your business card in it by mail
4) Talk on the phone and exchange ideas using Skype.
5) Exchange information and contracts by email.
6) Close a deal in person once all the paperwork is in place.

All these electronic and Internet sites can help you deal with at least half the approach needed to close a new deal, reduce costs and are often actually free. Results can be nearly instant and above all, customers expect companies to use the very latest technology. Mastering electronic communications is actually something which raises the prestige of your business and is a public relations goal in itself.

Step 5 – Getting the Deal

So far, we've researched our market, looked around for the right places to find leads, contacted them and made a gentle pitch, and above all, we've warmed up a few great prospects that would be happy to hear from us again. Next, it's time to make the pitch, be active and try to close a deal.

- The first stage is often the phone call. Get them on the phone or better still, arrange a visit or a meeting in person. You need to present your service or product in some unique way and never rely on documents alone to close a deal. So initially, your aim is to set up some way to get that close, personal contact you need.

Grow Your Business Using Biblical Principles™

- Next, as you open the call - be personal. Tell them what you did last night. Ask them how they are. Find out what is happening in their lives. Building a rapport is the best way to make the rest of the pitch go smoothly. Each time you contact a lead rapport is important, and here at the very end of the process, *it is vital*. You need enough rapport to smooth things through until a deal is made and motivate your lead on a personal level to do business with you.

- Finally, move onto what you want. This is the meat of the pitch. Be concise, be clear and have a call to action. Explain your pitch and idea; explain why you have chosen to tell this particular contact and then to close the deal, make your play for what you need. This could be a contract, a deal, an agreement, a payment, whatever suits your business model.

Pitching is an art form, but if you have done your homework and gone through each step of the process correctly, the pitch should merely be a way of collecting together everything you have set in motion and reaping the rewards. A good product or service, well marketed and properly explained to a lead who likes you, will sell itself if you close things professionally.

Everyone has some fear of rejection, so a 'no' might seem like a terrible thing to experience. The truth is that there must be a lot of 'no's' normally to find a 'yes' amongst them. It is critical not to be put off or distracted by a very emotional response to leads who say no. Remember, a 'no' isn't personal and is part of the normal daily life of enterprise. Every "No" is one step closer to "Yes"!

Another thing to note is that a 'no' may not be an outright 'no', and may in fact be a negative response only in the particular circumstances at the time. Often, you will yield good results by dealing with a 'no' professionally and checking what it means.

Here's an example of a pitch which seemingly results in an outright no, but can be rectified by asking the right questions towards the end.

- "Joe, let me tell what I want to accomplish to see if you can help me. I want to meet with you or someone in your company to share what we do, and to see if we would be a good fit. I hope you could help me to understand your organization, how you are structured. All I need is a half hour meeting. I don't want to waste your time. As an accountant, a bean counter, I know the value of time. Can you help me out??

-   *No, not right now. No I'm not interested....*

    Is that because this is close to the year end for taxes? I thought so....Look, it's clear that my business could help you but this just isn't the right time. Can we keep in contact??...Yes? Great I will speak to you again in three months...."

- 'No's' will get you to a yes until it is very clear that there is no hope or chance of this prospect ever doing business with you. You must find out directly where they are in the process as it relates to your offering. Some may disagree with me on this, but you need to know where they are in the decision making process. You need to stay on the prospect and follow-up regularly. By doing this, you shorten the sales cycle. Timing is everything. You don't know what they are going through, so one day you may call and they may be ready to buy. A strong rapport will build long term bonds which you can use to gently keep prospects rolling along until the right opportunity for a sale presents itself.

- Keep repeating one of the most valuable maxims in business - "The number of no's that you are willing to go through to get to your desired results will dictate whether or not you are successful." Most people are not afraid of the actual sales process, they are afraid of the rejection, the dreaded 'no'. Never be afraid of "no's", because they are a step towards a yes. Part of the skill in being in business is to know who *not* to trade with. A no is a big help in focusing your efforts in the right place.

Step 6 - The Black Hole of Voicemail

Voicemail can be a black hole. You may keep leaving messages but nothing seems to come of your efforts. Remember that voicemail is never an end in itself; you don't win business because a customer ever acts on a message, you win business by getting a return call and closing deals personally. Messages are a means to an end. In fact, this can be applied to all forms of messages in business. Voicemails, texts and even emails are all simply vehicles for moving a deal along until you can close it live.

Voicemail and its counterparts are still vital components in running a smooth business, so bear in mind two key precepts when you leave messages:

- Be persistent, but know when to quit. Keep calling until you hit 7-10 voicemails, at different times or days. In my experience, this is the limit for most people and ensures you give every prospect a really determined shot. You have nothing to lose by being persistent and if you are brief and to the point each time, you can reduce your expenditure of time even with a lot of prospects.

- Always leave creative messages and never be dull. Just like an actual phone call, you are building rapport. You need to charm and intrigue leads to induce them to want to call you back. For example, by leaving very strong value propositions, explaining you saved large dollar amounts for a similar client in Texas, you may get a client to phone back to see how the value proposition could be applied for their business. Or you can take a humorous approach, for example, "Don't waste my time, I speak to God more and he gets back to me. Why not you? This is my last voicemail... OK, I gave in and called you again".

- Finally, keep track of your appointments, calls and your other proposal materials and make sure you are keeping regular communications going. Send emails, letters and cards to keep in touch. Don't rely on your memory. Follow through with a customer relationship management program such as salesforce or ACT to track all activity. This will allow you to review when you last got in touch with the prospect and ensures that you keep everything flowing smoothly towards a sale.

I can recommend these techniques, which may not immediately appeal to you, because my feeling is that you have nothing to lose by focusing on persistence and creativity.

Not everyone will become your client and it is important to go out of any sales situation with your pride intact. So be firm, be persistent and be creative, and remember above all, the goal of the voicemail is to get a return call...

Step 7 – Keep Contacting

Stay in touch with your leads. You might not have closed the deal this time, but future business is much easier with a warm contact. Moreover, customers' needs and circumstances change over time, so it is important to stay connected to find out what is happening at all times.

As with voicemails and messages, any ongoing communication needs to be properly presented and designed to stimulate your leads. For example:

- Send e-mail newsletters with relevant industry news each month; send them a cookie when you know it is their birthday. Send them a letter when you read about them in the news.

- Send them a report on their industry. Giving away something of value, especially if produced in-house or which is an example of your work is a great way to build relationships through assistance.

- Get in touch with potential clients at least once every month. My belief is that this is the ideal frequency for approaching a lead and keeping his or her awareness of your business high over the long term.

Remember to respond to any questions or inquiries which arise, and keep things interesting with lots of variety in your methods. As well as direct customer contact, you should keep in contact with the whole market using public relations, advertising and word of mouth.

In fact, the best way to stay in touch is through the recommendations of others. If you can show your contacts the strength of your business proposition and the solid faith which bestows confidence – they will be sure to tell others. And there is nothing like people doing your arduous selling for you. There is no more powerful motivator of sales than personal recommendations so be sure to look after clients and your market alike to get the best out of this.

Chapter Sixteen – The Right Connections

Having the right connections and having the right people in your life is important, whether they are business contacts or members of your personal circle. Having divine connections can get you to the next level and change your life, both spiritually and materially, at work, in your business, and with your family. Remember that having the wrong people in your life, the wrong connections, and the wrong influencers is to surround yourself with naysayers. Naysayers are always a hindrance to receiving all the good things God has in store for you.

There are many people who have the right connections that will lead them to where they want to be. Imagine using your gifts for ministry, and needing a door opened so that you can be used by God in the gifting that you carry. Imagine getting connected to that one person who could get your career or business to a level that you never imagined. These critical links all come from God.

Making the right connections is a combination of finding the true people you need and minimizing the impact of negative influences.

I. A Proactive Approach

God is the one that can make things really happen for a business, but you have to take the initiative, stir the waters, and get out so that God can guide you to the right person and the right connection. Use the gifts in whatever setting is available in order to move the heavens in your favor. Get your guidance from God and be proactive in your approach and these major contacts will begin to fall into your lap.

Gilbert Pagan

I have been asked by many people, "How do I identify my giftings?" I tell them to look at what they are brutally good at, fanatical at – to find areas in which there is no competition for their gifts. Then, flow from that, flow in that anointing, and use the power and fire and passion that come with it. Flow in that teaching, preaching, selling, networking, whatever it is, flow in that and find at the end of this process your true giftings.

If you are brutally good at something, see if you can kick in a door for yourself. The right connection will not miraculously knock on your door, unless you throw some bread on the water. The bread needs to be thrown out there so that it will come back to you. You have to use the gift so that it can be seen, talked about, and for God to start moving people, situations and mountains in your favor.

II. Profiting From Connections

Proverbs 13:20 says *"He who walks with the wise, grows wise, but a companion of fools, suffers harm."*

Having the right people in your life, having people who are operating at a higher level than you spiritually, or in your career, or business, will make you raise your game and move you up the ladder.

- The right people in your life will allow for opportunities to flow and come your way. Having passionate people in your life will allow you to get passionate and on fire for God with power and anointing. This will flow to all areas of your life.

- Having people in your life that fast and pray, will make you do the same. Having people in your life that have hunger for the presence of God through prayer and service will make you hungry for God.

The right connections matter, relationships in your life matter. The people who run in your inner circle matter. Those that espouse your belief systems, your values, and speak your language, matter. Power, anointing, fire, fasting and praying lead to success and prosperity. Whatever that means for you, these are the right people and right connections that should be in your life.

Watch who is in your circle, who pours the spirit into you. See who prays for you, who gives you counsel. I am very careful to watch who is in my inner circle, who prays for me and lays hands on me.

I don't want anyone laying hands on me that has more issues and is worse off than I am.

I want someone praying for me who fasts, prays, has power and anointing - that is the right connection that I want pouring into me. Your friends and relationships influence you, so walk with the wise, find and attract people who are on a higher level, people on and above your level, holy and sanctified people. Discover and cultivate people that will keep you straight like a bowling ball going down the alley. They will serve as your bumper guards that will not let you go into the gutter.

III. Avoiding Naysayers

This was shared earlier, but worth repeating. Stay away from naysayers, stay away from people who say you can't do something in business or for God. They say they tried it, that it won't work. They may be well meaning, but they are on their own journey and may confuse their journey with yours.

God has your journey planned out. God at times will use other people, non-believers as well, to help you get on the right path to get to the right connections.

I used to work at a restaurant in NYC for about 4 years, this was about 25 years ago and I had not gone to college yet. I was trying to find myself. There was customer named Lenny. He was a textile salesman and he sold comforters to Macy's and Bloomingdales. He made a lot of money. At least it appeared that way to me at that time.

He saw in me the ability to go to college. He saw that I was smart, and in essence he believed in me, and told me, "Your communication, people and sales skills are being wasted in the restaurant business."

There is nothing wrong with the restaurant business. But it was not for me. Shortly thereafter I went to college, worked for corporate America for about 20 years then started my own business.

This was a divine connection placed in my path to guide me. I was sensitive to it, listening for God's voice, and did not miss God talking. Sometimes we get caught up in the noise of life and our radio station has static, and God is talking but we are not listening.

"Divine connections don't only open doors, they also guide you."

For many, learning to say 'no' and to walk away from naysayers will take practice, but by learning how to be firm and stay-positive, you will often leave these people trailing in your wake.

IV. Christian Business Networks

There are Christian business organizations all around the world. Many have seminars, conferences and forums where you can meet and network with other like-minded businesspeople. They are an ideal beginning to building the right connections.

The CBMC is the Christian Businessman's Connection, a global network based in Chattanooga, with both management and field ministry divisions. They help organize meetings and aim to encourage Christians to find people who can help their business grow while remaining true to their principles.

Another example is the CLA, the Christian Leadership Alliance, based at Azusa Pacific University. Their work is geared towards both profit making and non-profit business leaders, helping to guide them through learning, developing resources and bringing the right people together.

There are lots of these places to find contacts, both just around the corner, and across the globe. Keep your head up and eyes open!

Chapter Seventeen - Questions & Activities

To get the most from this book, it is vital that you look to yourself, your own business and your own life. To help, here are some questions and activities which will pull Christian thinking and Biblical principles into your daily life.

Take a moment to work through them. Be honest and answer from your heart. Write your answers down and a day or two later revisit them. Try to know yourself, studying your own answers to find better ways to use the Bible in daily life.

I. Personal

- How long have you been a believer?
- What motivated you and continues to motivate you?
- What lessons do you learn from the Scriptures?
- How do you apply these in daily life?

II. Business

- How does your faith influence your business?

Grow Your Business Using Biblical Principles™

- How does you values affect how you do business, the deals you make etc.?

- Do you share your faith and business values with your employees?

- What are your thoughts on developing a Facebook fan page, and getting leads from Facebook? Or LinkedIn?

- What Goliaths have you faced and how have you overcome them? How do you plan to overcome them in the future?

- How do you spread your message? Is it a clear message?

- What is your plan and goals for the business?

- How could you practice more Christian thinking in your day to day working life?

If you need help in growing your business and would like a God centered approach, connect with us.

Lease A Sales Rep
www.LeaseASalesRep.com

Made in the USA
San Bernardino, CA
01 January 2016